Understanding The New Testament
An Introductory Atlas

Paul H. Wright

cartaJerusalem

Contents

List of Maps

Copyright © 2004
Carta Jerusalem, Ltd.
18 Ha'uman Street, P.O.B. 2500, Jerusalem 9102401, Israel
www.carta-jerusalem.com
E-mail: carta@carta.co.il

Cartography: Carta, Jerusalem

Photographs: Paul H. Wright

Photograph on page 21 (bottom): Cindy van Volsem
Reconstruction on page 29: Leen Ritmeyer

ISBN: 965-220-525-7

Printed in Israel

Printing
10 9 8 7 6 5

(opposite) The Sea of Galilee at sunset.

For Hardin Wright,
in his ninth decade as a student of the Bible,
and his grandchildren, who are beginning

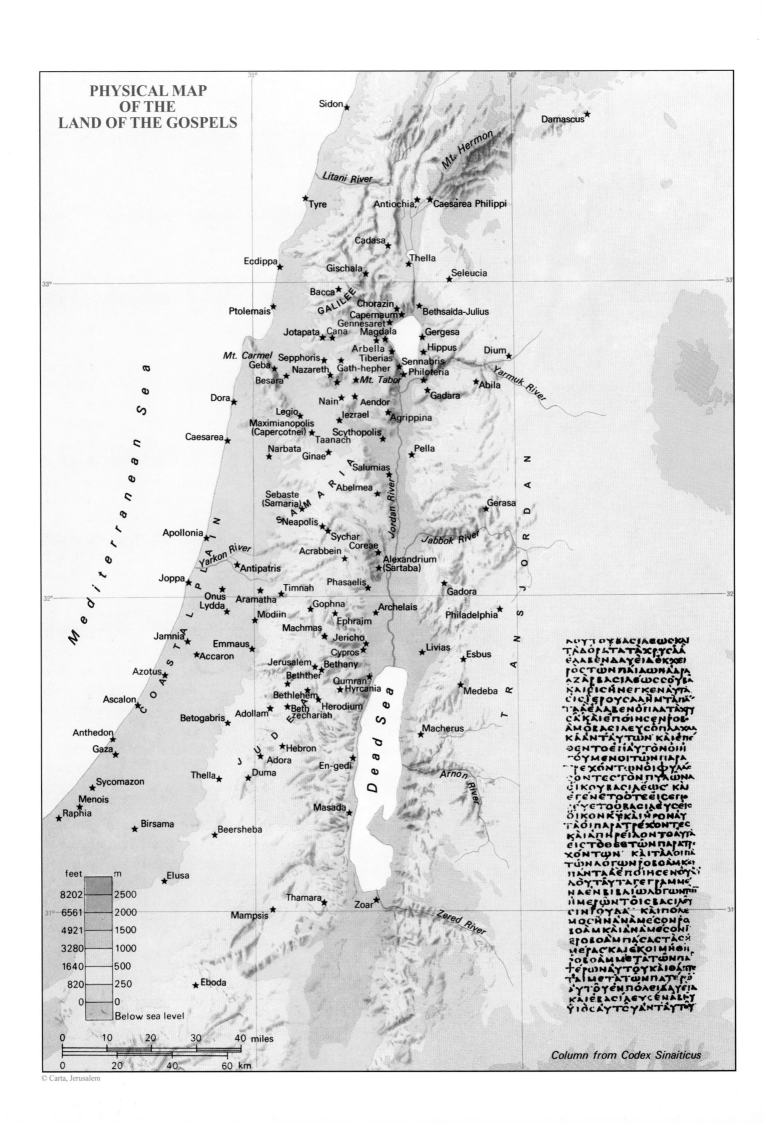

PHYSICAL MAP OF THE LAND OF THE GOSPELS

Sidon

Damascus

Mt. Hermon

Litani River

Tyre
Antiochia
Caesarea Philippi

Cadasa
Thella
Seleucia

Ecdippa
Gischala

Bacca
GALILEE
Chorazin
Bethsaida-Julius

Ptolemais
Capernaum
Gennesaret
Gergesa
Jotapata
Cana
Magdala
Hippus

Mt. Carmel
Sepphoris
Arbella
Tiberias
Dium
Geba
Nazareth
Gath-hepher
Sennabris
Philoteria
Yarmuk River
Besara
Mt. Tabor
Abila

Dora
Nain
Aendor
Gadara

Legio
Iezrael
Agrippina
Maximianopolis
(Capercotnei)
Scythopolis

Caesarea
Taanach

Narbata
Pella
Ginae

Salumias

Abelmea
Jordan River
SAMARIA
Sebaste
(Samaria)
Gerasa

Neapolis
Sychar
Coreae
Jabbok River
Apollonia
Acrabbein
Alexandrium
(Sartaba)

Yarkon River
Antipatris

Joppa
Phasaelis
Gadora

Timnah
Onus
Aramatha
Gophna
Archelais
Philadelphia
Lydda
Modiin
Ephrajm

Jamnia
Machmas
Jericho
Livias
Emmaus
Esbus
Accaron
Cypros

Azotus
Jerusalem
Bethany
Bethther
Qumran
Medeba

Ascalon
Bethlehem
Hyrcania
Herodium
Betogabris
Adollam
Beth-
zechariah
Anthedon
JUDEA
Macherus
Gaza
Hebron

Thella
Adora
En-gedi
Arnon River
Sycomazon
Duma
Menois
Raphia
Masada
Birsama
Beersheba

Mediterranean Sea
COASTAL PLAIN
Dead Sea
TRANS JORDAN

Elusa

Thamara
Zoar
Mampsis
Zered River

Eboda

feet	m
8202	2500
6561	2000
4921	1500
3280	1000
1640	500
820	250
0	0
	Below sea level

0 10 20 30 40 miles

0 20 40 60 km

Column from Codex Sinaiticus

© Carta, Jerusalem

The New Testament: Text and Context

The Christian Scriptures are composed of the New Testament (containing 27 books), the Old Testament (with 39 books, counted as 24 in the Hebrew Bible) and, in the Catholic tradition, the Apocrypha (usually numbering 15 books). Written by a handful of men over the course of several decades in the mid- to late first century A.D., the New Testament contains a record (or, more properly, multiple records) of the life of Jesus Christ and the birth and early growth of Christianity. Although each of the books of the New Testament possesses a character and flavor of its own, the group as a whole is unified around a single overarching theme: Jesus of Nazareth is the long-awaited Jewish Messiah, and because of his life, death and resurrection the community of people who believe in him (the Church) can find favor with God.

The New Testament was written in Koine Greek, the common dialect of the vast Greek-speaking world of the first century A.D. This allowed the writings of the New Testament to be read and understood widely, and the Gospel, or "good news" of Jesus Christ, to be carried throughout the Mediterranean basin and beyond. However, linguistic and literary evidence found in Matthew, Mark and Luke suggest that at least these three gospels (the Synoptic or "look-alike" gospels) may have been written first in Hebrew, and were rooted deeply in the Jewish world of first-century Palestine.

For two thousand years, Bible readers have looked to the words of the New Testament to find meaning and direction for life. Those who seek to understand the message that it holds for today quickly come to realize that it is also important to study its original context, the world in which the authors of the New Testament lived and wrote. Questions related to the meaning of a passage, its style and idiom, are clarified by looking at the larger literary context within which the passage appears (the paragraph, chapter or New Testament book in which it is found, and the Bible as a whole), but also by considering background of the text itself. Why was a gospel or epistle written, and for whom? What specific need was the author trying to address? What did he assume his original audience already knew? Why did he choose to say what he did in the way that he did?

An important part of context is place. For all of the relative ease of travel that characterized the Roman world of the first century A.D., most people stayed pretty close to home. The role that a person's hometown played in defining his or her personal, social and religious identity cannot be overestimated. A Jewish peasant farmer living high in the hill country of Judea viewed the world quite differently than did an urban gentile born and raised on the edge of the Aegean Sea. A Hellenized Jew from Alexandria, a religious Jew from western Galilee and a villager native to Galatia were all part of the larger Roman and New Testament world; while each sought peace, security and the good life for himself and his family, each defined what that meant in very different ways.

The New Testament was written by, to and about real people living in real places. The writers of the New Testament had an intimate knowledge of place, and of the particular challenges that living in this or that place held for life. Moreover, the events and images described by the writers of the New Testament are grounded in an assumed knowledge of particular places or of specific aspects of the geographical or physical world in which individuals lived. The lands of the Bible have been aptly described as the "stage" on which the people who grace the pages of the New Testament moved, or as the "playing board" for which the "instructions" for people living there (the New Testament itself) were given. By understanding the dynamic of place, we open a window into other aspects of personal and communal life: political, economic, social and religious.

In looking at the world of the New Testament, many Bible readers focus on the words of the Apostle Paul found in Galatians 4:4: "But when the fullness of time had come, God sent forth his Son. ..." The phrase "fullness of time" points to the religious, social, and cultural conditions that fostered the rise and spread of Christianity, first in Palestine and then in the Greco-Roman world. But it is also proper to speak of a "fullness of place," of the geographical realities of the first-century world in which the Gospel spread. By learning about these places and the historical interconnections between them, Bible readers can enter more deeply into the pages of the Bible and the divine message that it contains.

The Books of the New Testament

Historical Books (The Gospels and Acts)

Matthew. In several ways, the Gospel of Matthew bridges the gap between the world of the Old Testament and that of the New. First, the book opens with a genealogy of Jesus that is tied into the royal line of Judah. Second, the author repeatedly states that Jesus fulfilled Old Testament messianic prophecies. Third, with a geographical sweep that includes everything from Mesopotamia (the visit of the Magi) to Egypt (the flight of the Holy family), the Gospel implies that the world of Abraham and his descendants (cf. Gen 11:31–12:10) has become the world of Jesus and his followers. Five major discourses by Jesus dominate the book, suggesting that the divine word has once again come to the people of the land of Israel. The book's author, Matthew (also called Levi—cf. Mk 2:14), a tax-collector from Capernaum, became one of the twelve Apostles.

Mark. The Gospel of Mark, which begins with the baptism rather than the birth of Jesus, is a fast-moving, tightly packed account of Jesus' ministry in Galilee that culminates in his journey to Jerusalem and the cross. Throughout, the gospel focuses on action rather than word, noting Jesus' ready ability to rub shoulders with his fellow countrymen and meet whatever needs they might have. The book's author, Mark (also called John Mark—cf. Acts 12:12), a man who may have had family ties to Jerusalem, was a long-time traveling companion of the Apostle Paul (2 Tim 4:11).

Luke. The Gospel of Luke is the most universal of the gospels in scope, covering the sweep of Jesus' life from conception to resurrection and following his journeys throughout Judea, Samaria, Galilee and the surrounding regions. Luke's gospel includes a number of stories not mentioned by the other gospels (ch. 9–18). Of particular note is Luke's emphasis on marginalized or peripheral elements of Jewish society: women, lepers, and foreigners. That the book's author, Luke, was a well-educated physician (cf. Col 4:14) is attested by the gospel's heart-felt compassion and attention to detail.

John. As the last gospel written, John presents the most complete picture of Jesus' humanity and his divinity. Selected events from Jesus' Galilean and early Jerusalem ministries (ch. 1–11) serve to provide the background for his climactic last week in Jerusalem (ch. 12–21). Because John mentions three Passover festivals (2:13; 6:4; 11:55), most interpreters conclude that Jesus' public ministry lasted three years. The book's author, John the son of Zebedee (cf. Mt 4:21), was a Galilean fisherman who became Jesus' closest disciple (cf. Jn 19:26) and one of the most prominent Apostles.

The Acts of the Apostles. Following Jesus' charge that his disciples should be his witnesses "both in Jerusalem, and in all Judea, and in Samaria, and unto the uttermost part of the earth" (1:8), the Acts of the Apostles tracks the earliest years of Christianity from Jerusalem to Rome. On the way, disciples such as Peter, Stephen, Philip and Paul (Saul of Tarsus) carry the Gospel message to a variety of Jewish and gentile audiences. Based on style and content, it is reasonable to conclude that Acts was written by Luke.

Epistles

Romans. The Apostle Paul's greatest epistle was written to the local church in Rome, a church that held a special place in his heart even though it was founded by someone else. For Paul, the fact that there were disciples of Jesus in Rome—the world's bastion of wealth, imperial might, and paganism—was proof of the power of the Gospel. Paul's epistle to the Romans is a well-reasoned argument of how the death and resurrection of Jesus provides justification and righteousness for all who have faith in him. Paul concludes his epistle by urging the church in Rome to demonstrate their new-found righteousness by their deeds.

1 and 2 Corinthians. Paul founded the church at Corinth during his second missionary journey (cf. Acts 18:1–17). The church grew significantly during his 18-month stay in Corinth, and counted among its members Crispus, the leader of the local synagogue (cf. Acts 18:8). But Corinth was a bustling seaport dominated both by the rougher elements of life and the appeal of Greco-Roman paganism, aspects of life that for the Corinthian church were too seductive. Paul's first letter to the Corinthians, probably written when he was at Ephesus on his third missionary journey, addresses a number of these problems and urges the Corinthian Christians to live lives worthy of the love of Christ. Paul's second letter to the Corinthians expresses his joy upon hearing that many Corinthian believers had turned from following teachers who had maligned him, and urges that his authority be acknowledged by the rest.

Galatians. Paul's epistle to the Galatians was written to churches sprinkled throughout Galatia, the high mountainous interior of Asia Minor, including those he founded on his first missionary journey (Antioch, Iconium, Lystra and Derbe; cf. Acts 13–14). Written before he penned his epistle to the Romans, Galatians can be considered Paul's primer on justification by faith, arguing that righteousness before God is based on grace, not works.

Ephesians. Paul spent nearly three years in Ephesus (cf. Acts 20:31), an important commercial city on the Aegean coast of the Roman province of Asia. His subsequent letter to the Ephesians—which was probably intended to be circulated among churches throughout Asia—is a mature treatise on the blessings and responsibilities of living the Christian life.

Philippians. Philip of Macedon, father of Alexander the Great, founded the city of Philippi on a fertile plain just north of the Aegean Sea. By the first century AD Philippi was one of the most important cities in northeastern Macedonia, and it was here that Paul planted the first church on European soil (cf. Acts 16). Paul enjoyed an especially close relationship with this church, and his letter to the Philippians, written when he was in prison in Rome, radiates his joy and confidence in their life in Christ.

Colossians. Colossae was a rather insignificant town lying in the Lycus River valley, nestled in a beautiful mountainous area in southwestern Asia Minor one hundred miles east of Ephesus. Previously an important commercial center, by the first century A.D. the city had been eclipsed by the nearby cities of Laodicea and Hierapolis (cf. Col 4:13). The epistle to the church at Colossae, as well as that to the church at Laodicea (Col 4:16), were intended to be read in churches throughout the region. Although the Apostle Paul never visited Colossae, he knew its church well enough to direct his letter against a syncretistic heresy which threatened his teaching on the uniqueness of Christ.

Mountains edging the Lycus Valley, viewed from the mound of Colossae.

1 and 2 Thessalonians. Paul's first two epistles were written to the church at Thessalonica, the capital of Macedonia and an important Aegean port city on the Egnatian Way, Rome's principle highway to the east. Paul founded the Thessalonian church on his second missionary journey (cf. Acts 17:1–9), but had to flee the city in the face of persecution before the church had a chance to grow in its faith. Later during his journey, perhaps when he was in Corinth, Paul wrote his first epistle to the church in Thessalonica, a wide-ranging, practical letter aimed at encouraging the church to continue to mature in spite of ongoing persecution and to answer questions about the second coming of Christ. In his second letter, Paul corrects certain misunderstandings about Christ's second coming which had arisen from comments he had made in his first.

1 and 2 Timothy. Timothy, whose mother was Jewish and father was Greek, came to faith in Christ in his home church of Lystra (cf. Acts 16:1–2), a city in southern Galatia. As Paul passed through the city on his second missionary journey, Timothy joined the apostle on his travels. Timothy remained a faithful and committed traveling companion of Paul and eventually spent significant time as the young pastor of the influential church in Ephesus (1 Tim 1: 3). Paul's first letter to Timothy warns against unorthodox teaching and provides instruction for administering the growing Ephesian church. His second letter, written while awaiting execution in a Roman prison, urges Timothy to remain strong and, if possible, travel to Rome to visit his aging spiritual father.

Titus. Titus, who was Greek, was a tireless traveling companion of Paul. He served Paul as an ecclesiastical trouble-shooter, going to Corinth and Crete to sort out problems in the churches there (cf. 2 Cor 8:6, 16–17; Titus 1:5). Titus's travels also took him as far as Dalmatia (modern Croatia and Bosnia; cf. 2 Tim 4:10) and Jerusalem (Gal 2:1). Paul's pastoral epistle to Titus urges Titus to appoint qualified leaders for the Cretan church, preach sound doctrine and encourage good works.

Philemon. Philemon was a well-to-do resident of Colossae who offered his home as a meeting place for the local church there. He was also a slave owner, and one of his slaves, Onesimus, had run away to Rome after causing Philemon financial harm, only to come to faith in Christ under the ministry of Paul. Paul's letter to Philemon, a window into issues of domestic concern, urges him to accept Onesimus back as a Christian brother.

Hebrews. The epistle to the Hebrews, an anonymous book, reflects a stage in the development of the early Church in which the Church was starting to pull away from Judaism. The author argues that the revelation of God through Jesus was superior to that of angels, prophets and even Moses himself. For this reason, believers in Jesus should hold fast to what they have been taught and, like the great men and women of the Old Testament, remain faithful to the end in spite of persecution. This epistle was apparently written to Jewish believers in Jesus, but their location, whether in Israel or the Roman world, is unknown, and the letter is largely lacking in geographical information.

James. The epistle of James, more a sermon than a letter, was written to "the twelve tribes in the dispersion" (1:1), a broad reference to Jewish believers in Jesus scattered across the known world. This universal audience is matched by the universal theme of the letter, namely, that faith, or belief in God, is useless without an accompanying display of faithfulness, i.e., good works. Tradition holds that the author of this epistle was James the brother of Jesus (cf. Mk 6:3), who became the head of the Jerusalem church (cf. Acts 15:13). This is supported by the large number of teachings in the book that parallel the words of Jesus.

1 and 2 Peter. The first epistle of Peter, a Bethsaida-born fisherman turned chief Apostle, was written to "pilgrims of the dispersion" in Pontus, Galatia, Cappadocia, Asia and Bithynia, districts in northern and western Asia Minor (1:1). Peter wrote from "Babylon" (5:13), a cryptic allusion to Rome, where tradition holds he was martyred. In this letter, Peter urges his audience to stand fast in the face of persecution. Peter's second epistle, written to Christians generally, warns against the dangers of false prophets and speaks of future judgment at the second coming of Christ.

1, 2 and 3 John. Identified only as "the Elder" in 2 and 3 John and not at all in 1 John, early Church tradition has long held that the writer of these epistles was Jesus' beloved disciple John, author of the fourth gospel. According to this tradition, John became the leader of the church in Ephesus after the fall of Jerusalem. John writes as a loving elder statesman, building on the teachings of his gospel and prompting his readers to love each other with the fellowship and love of Christ.

Jude. Tradition holds that Jude's epistle was written by Judas the brother of Jesus and James (cf. Mk 6:3). There is no geographical information in Jude's letter which would help to identify its audience, nor is it clear whether Jude was writing to Jewish believers in Jesus or gentile Christians. Jude refers to several events—some from the Old Testament and others known only from Jewish apocalyptic literature—to illustrate the danger of following false teachers and accepting their aberrant, almost fantastic, beliefs.

Prophecy

The Revelation of John. The Apocalypse (or, "Revelation") of John was written to Christians "to show things which must shortly take place" (Rev 1:1). The language throughout is cryptic, symbolic and highly graphic, apparently intended to conceal as well as to reveal. The author, the Apostle John, Jesus' beloved disciple, draws heavily on imagery from the Old Testament and Jewish apocalyptic literature as he describes terrible trials which will someday face the Church. John opens his book with a personal challenge to seven churches in western Asia (Ephesus, Smyrna, Pergamum, Thyatira, Sardis, Philadelphia and Laodicea), and ends with a glorious picture of a new heaven and new earth, a new Jerusalem that brings the perfection of Eden to the now triumphant universal Church.

The Land of the Gospels

The land of the Gospels—the land that Jesus walked—is a narrow strip wedged between the Mediterranean Sea and the upper reaches of the vast Arabian Desert. The great trunk road that has connected Mesopotamia and Egypt since antiquity bisects this land from north to south. During the time of the Old Testament this road brought the merchants and armies of the world's great empires to the doorstep of ancient Israel. By the time of the New Testament the geopolitical center of the world had shifted westward to the Aegean and Rome, and the homeland of the Jews was reduced to a far-flung corner of the Roman Empire. Nevertheless, Jesus' travels in his ancestral land brought him into contact with peoples representing everything that the Roman world had to offer.

The land of the Gospels can be divided into five basic geopolitical divisions: Judea, Samaria, the Coastal Plain, Galilee, and Transjordan. For comparative purposes, the modern state of Israel, including the West Bank, is about the same size as New Jersey and slightly smaller than Wales. Yet this small region contains a variety of landforms and changes in climate similar to that found in California. Far from uniform in shape, style and substance, the land of the Gospels provides a fitting stage for the weave of stories of the New Testament world.

Judea

The heartland of Judea consists of the rugged limestone hill country lying within a day's walk of Jerusalem. Elevations reaching over 900 meters (2,950 feet) provide the land with cold, wet winters and summers that, though sunny and hot, are usually cooled by mid-afternoon Mediterranean breezes. With the primary exceptions of the city of Jerusalem and the town that grew up next to Herod's winter palace at Jericho, this was a land of villages and farms, with terraces of grapevines and olive, fig and pomegranate trees embracing the hills. The land's ruggedness tended to isolate the people of Judea from its more open neighbors on every side, fostering a degree of conservatism more prevalent here than in the surrounding regions.

Dropping out of the hill country to the east, one encounters the chalky wilderness of Judea, an arid land best suited for flocks of sheep and goats. Beyond is the Dead Sea, the lowest spot and saltiest body of water on the face of the earth. On its western shore, between Jericho and En-gedi, grew the Roman world's supply of balsam.

To the west of the hill country the broad valleys of the Shephelah, or foothills, open the land of Judea to the coastal plain. Here conditions are favorable for agriculture, and the alluvial soil, ample rainfall and warmer overall temperatures prove ideal for fields of wheat and barley. In the days of the New Testament the southern section of the Shephelah was called Idumea, with a population that traced its roots to the Edomites, descendants of Esau who settled there after the fall of the Old Testament kingdom of Judah.

Samaria

In terms of soil and water—its best natural resources—the hill coun-

Olive trees on the terraced hillsides of Judea.

Northern Samaria, viewed from Mount Gilboa.

try of Samaria surpasses that of its southern Judean neighbor. This was the region of the Old Testament tribes of Ephraim and Manasseh, a land that the biblical writers described as the most blessed of all the tribal inheritances (Gen 49:22–26; Deut 33:13–17). It was also the heartland of the northern kingdom of Israel. Elevations in Samaria rarely exceed 750 meters (2,460 feet), which results in moderate wintertime temperatures. A network of broad alluvial valleys run through the center of the hill country, giving Samaria a mixed and fertile economic base. The natural routes connecting these valleys also join Samaria to the outside world, opening its people to foreign religious and cultural influences. Samaria's population in the first century was mixed Samaritan and gentile, and Jews traveling between Jerusalem and Galilee preferred to avoid the region altogether.

The Coastal Plain

A broad, north-south plain separates the hill country of Judea and Samaria from the Mediterranean Sea. Here rich alluvial soils washed down from the hills mix with North African sand, brought ashore by the continual action of current and waves. The southern part of the plain (Old Testament Philistia) is a flat, fertile agricultural land that has always supported a relatively large population and, from the beginning of the historic period, true cities. In the north (the Sharon Plain), several long, low ridges of *kurkar* (solidified sand dunes) parallel the shore, impeding the flow of runoff water to the coast and resulting in a relatively soggy land that never attracted a large population.

The international flavor of the Coastal Plain is primarily a result of the land route connecting Egypt with Asia and Europe that runs its length, and by the time of the New Testament the cultural influences of Hellenism were well entrenched along its length. In contrast,

the plain's long, gently arched coastline, with no decent breaks to form a natural harbor except at Joppa (modern Tel Aviv), failed to draw the populations of Judea and Samaria into the Mediterranean world. Eventually Herod's massive man-made harbor at Caesarea remedied this, and provided the region the necessary port to interact freely with the West.

Galilee

Galilee, a diverse region in the northern part of the land of the Gospels, was the focal point of most of Jesus' ministry. The region is separated from the hills of Samaria by the vast Jezreel Valley, a geological basin which serves not only as the agricultural breadbasket of the entire area but also as a wide-open corridor channeling international traffic between West and East, between the lands of the Mediterranean and those of Transjordan. Jesus' boyhood home of Nazareth was located high on a limestone ridge overlooking the Jezreel Valley from the north; no doubt the valley's rich and storied history helped to shape his messianic awareness.

The limestone hills of Galilee are high and rugged in the north (over 600 meters/1,970 feet, hence the term "Upper Galilee"), and lower in the south ("Lower Galilee"). Upper Galilee resembles the higher parts of the hill country of Judea in many respects, particularly in its agricultural base and general isolation from the larger world around, although Upper Galilee is wetter and more productive. Lower Galilee is characterized by a series of parallel hilly ridges separated by broad, fertile valleys, and it is here that most of the population of first-century Galilee lived. The relatively low terrain of Lower Galilee makes for fairly easy travel throughout, and serves to pull the region together as a self-contained unit while at the same time linking it to its neighbors. Nestled among basalt hills to the east lies the jeweled Sea of Galilee, the only freshwater lake

The Golan region (ancient Gaulanitis) with Mount Hermon in the background.

of any consequence on the entire eastern Mediterranean seaboard and the primary natural resource of all of Galilee.

Transjordan

The lands of Transjordan are separated from Judea, Samaria and Galilee by the Rift Valley, a massive geological tear on the surface of the earth that extends from southern Turkey deep into East Africa. The northernmost part of Transjordan (today's Golan, opposite Galilee) is a well-watered area of basalt that rises eastward to form a high plateau that was intensively farmed for wheat in Roman times. To the south, and east of Samaria, looms the high limestone dome of Gilead with mountainous slopes terraced for grapevines, olives and figs. Farther south yet, above the Dead Sea, rises a chalky plateau best suited for grazing land, the homeland of the Old Testament kingdom of Moab. And in the deep south beyond lie the arid, high and somewhat mysterious mountains of Edom which, by the time of the New Testament, were dominated by the Nabateans, a kingdom of camel caravaneers who controlled the spice route coming out of the Arabian Peninsula. The lands of Transjordan are connected by an international highway, a landed eastern route paralleling that along the Mediterranean coast. The Roman Empire's southeastern frontier never pushed beyond Transjordan; farther east, the vast Arabian Desert lay untamed even by the power and resources of Rome.

Roman remains of Gerasa (modern Jerash), one of the cities of the Decapolis in Transjordan.

Peoples and Lands of the New Testament World

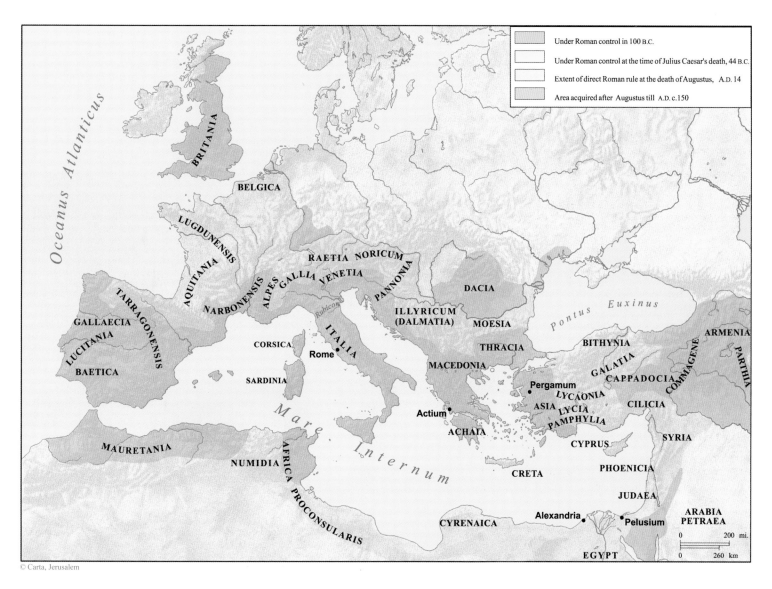

▨	Under Roman control in 100 B.C.
☐	Under Roman control at the time of Julius Caesar's death, 44 B.C.
☐	Extent of direct Roman rule at the death of Augustus, A.D. 14
▨	Area acquired after Augustus till A.D. c.150

© Carta, Jerusalem

The world of the New Testament was a Mediterranean world. The march of Alexander the Great through the ancient Near East, from Macedonia to India, awoke the lands of the Old Testament to the emerging world of Hellenism, and eventually to Rome itself. With it, the center of the world swung west to the Mediterranean basin, bringing new social, economic and religious opportunities—and the accompanying challenges that followed close behind.

The lands of the ancient Near East hung along the Fertile Crescent, crowded by the looming mass of the Arabian Desert and balanced on either end by the river valleys of the Nile to the west and the Tigris and Euphrates to the east. By contrast, the Mediterranean basin was a vast amphitheater, a circle of lands and peoples drawn together by the closeness of the sea and protected from lands beyond by a wider, almost unbroken circle of mountain and desert. The peninsulas of Italy and Greece; the large islands of Cyprus, Crete and Sicily; a scattering of smaller islands filling the Aegean; innumerable bays, inlets, estuaries, seas and coves—these natural geographic features within the Mediterranean basin connected sea and land, providing an expanding network of routes that hurried both armies and commerce to the farthest corners of this new world. By the end of the first century A.D. the lands of the Mediterranean basked in Pax Romana, the "Peace of Rome," as the military priorities that build the Roman Empire gradually gave way to the social and economic benefits that came in its wake.

A list of peoples who visited Jerusalem for the Jewish festival of Shavuot (Pentecost) seven weeks after the crucifixion and resurrection of Jesus is found in Acts 2:9–11. This list is a sampling of lands and peoples of the Mediterranean—including a few from the ancient Near East—and provides a first-century "Table of Nations" (cf. Genesis 10) ripe for the spread of the Gospel. More Mediterranean lands are mentioned in other writings of the New Testament. Taken together, those that played the most prominent role in the story of the New Testament are listed below, in counterclockwise geographical order.

Syria (Syro-Phoenicia). The large Roman province of Syria encompassed most of what is today modern Syria and Lebanon, in addition to parts of southeastern Turkey (Asia Minor). During at least part of the time of the New Testament, Syria also exercised some control over Judea and Galilee (cf. Lk 2:1–2). The capital of Syria was Antioch, a beautifully situated city nestled near the northernmost bend of the Orontes River. It was here that the followers of Jesus were first called "Christians" (Acts 11:19–26; 15:22–23). Syria was an extremely hellenized part of the Roman Empire. Many established cities here had already been given Greek names during the Hellenistic period and were eventually rebuilt according to classic Greco-Roman architectural lines, becoming important centers of Greek philosophy and literature. Hellenism first gained a foothold in

Syria through cities such as Tyre and Sidon, old seafaring ports that hugged the rocky Phoenician (Lebanese) coast. In part the Greeks and Romans simply took advantage of the role that these cities had already played in the Mediterranean world, for by establishing trading colonies throughout the Mediterranean as early as the eighth century B.C., Tyre and Sidon had forged close economic and political ties with the west long before the rise of Rome.

Cyprus. Cyprus, an island rich in natural resources, is noted especially for its copper mines (which were controlled in the late first century B.C. by Herod the Great) and timber. On a clear day it is possible to see both southern Turkey and the Lebanese mountains from the northeastern part of the island, and this close proximity to the mainland made Cyprus a cultural crossroads in the eastern Mediterranean throughout antiquity. Tied to both Greece and Phoenicia from its earliest days, Cyprus lay astride some of the most active shipping lanes in the Mediterranean (cf. Acts 21:3, 27:4). Historically the island was inhabited by Minoans and then Greeks, and in intertestamental times was controlled alternatively by Persia, Ptolemaic Egypt, and Rome as each in turn sought to gain strategic advantage in the eastern Mediterranean. Apparently there was a large and vibrant Jewish population in Cyprus by the first century A.D.; there was, for instance, more than one synagogue at Salamis, the main port on the eastern side of the island (Acts 13: 4–5). Barnabas, a native of Cyprus (Acts 4:36), joined the Apostle Paul and John Mark on their first missionary journey, visiting synagogues the length of the island from Salamis to Paphos (Acts 13:4–6). When the island's procounsul Sergius Paulus embraced Christianity as a result of Paul's preaching, Cyprus became the first Roman territory to be governed by a Christian (Acts 13:6–12).

Cilicia. The province of Cilicia was located in Asia Minor at the northeastern corner of the Mediterranean Sea. A large, fertile plain dominated the eastern end of Cilicia, and was home to a thriving Greek and Jewish population at the time of the New Testament. The easternmost city on this plain, Issus, was the site of Alexander the Great's decisive battle against Darius the Persian in 333 B.C., which opened the east to Hellenism. Tarsus, on the western end of the plain, was a center of education rivaling Alexandria and Athens, and also the hometown of the Apostle Paul. Behind this plain towered the Taurus Mountains, a rugged 10,000-foot wall separating continental Asia from Asia Minor. These mountains were punctured by the narrow Cilician Gates, a formidable pass above Tarsus that carried most of the traffic between west and east. The Apostle Paul navigated the Cilician Gates on his second and third missionary journeys (Acts 15:41, 18:23).

Cappadocia. Cappadocia was a rugged, barren province in east central Asia Minor, occupying much of the heartland of the ancient Hittite Empire. Elevations up to 3,960 meters (13,000 feet) made for an extreme climate and harsh living conditions, and the hardy residents of Cappadocia, like their Hittite predecessors, raised mostly sheep and horses. Hellenism was not particularly attracted to these conditions, and the relatively small, largely rural population of Cappadocia tended to resist outside influences. Nevertheless, there were Jewish residents of Cappadocia, and "sojourners scattered throughout Cappadocia" were among the recipients of the first epistle of Peter (1 Pet 1:1).

Bithynia and Pontus. Bithynia and Pontus were originally two neighboring regions in northwestern Asia Minor lying along the southern coast of the Black Sea. Scant agricultural land, a noticeable lack of good harbors and frequent earthquakes conspired to hold back the progress of the area. In addition, high mountains in the south tended to isolate the coastal cities of Bithynia and Pontus from the interior of Asia Minor, and the tough inhabitants of these regions remained largely independent until they were incorporated into the Roman Empire as a single province in the first century B.C. Even though the Apostle Paul was "not permitted by the Spirit of Jesus" to visit Bithynia (Acts 16:7), the early Church did take root there (1 Pet 1:1), probably first among the regions' Jewish population which counted among its natives Aquila, one of Paul's closest companions (Acts 18:1; cf. Acts 2:9).

Galatia. In the third century B.C. bands of migrating Gauls from Europe settled on the high mountainous plateau of north central Asia Minor, establishing there the independent kingdom of Galatia. In 25 B.C. this kingdom, along with its mountainous southern neighbors Pisidia (Acts 14:24), Lycaonia (Acts 14:11) and parts of Phrygia (cf. Acts 2:10), were incorporated into the Roman Empire, becoming together the Roman province of Galatia. This was a wild and rugged land, inhabited—at least from the point of view of Rome—by people of a similar temperament. Neither Hellenism nor, it is assumed, Judaism, took deep root in the northern part of the province and fared only a little better in the south, and Rome's occupation throughout was primarily military. Nevertheless, the Apostle Paul traveled through the southern, Pisidian part of Galatia on all three of his missionary journeys, establishing a handful of churches there in spite of ongoing travel dangers (cf. 2 Cor 11:26). Timothy, perhaps Paul's favorite disciple, was a native of Lystra in Pisidian Galatia (Acts 16:1–2).

Pamphylia. The Roman province of Pamphylia consisted of an alluvial plain that followed the curve of a vast arc on the south Asia Minor coast tucked between two massive outcroppings of the Taurus Mountains, with Cilicia to the east and Lycia (Acts 27:5) to the west. With a pleasant year-round climate and ample water supplies, this fertile plain produced orchard and field crops in abundance, and supported five large Hellenistic port cities. Of these, the Apostle Paul passed through Perga (Acts 13:13–14) and Attalia (Acts 14:25; modern Antalya) on his first journey into Galatia. Squarely facing the Mediterranean, Pamphylia was home to a wide variety of peoples (the name Pamphylia means "of all peoples"), yet served more as a port for regional pirates than for cosmopolitan Rome. Even though Pamphylia had an established Jewish population (Acts 2:10), the New Testament records little of Paul's work to establish churches there.

Asia. The Roman province of Asia filled the entire western third of Asia Minor, including numerous islands off its coast. Asia was oriented westward, with several large rivers slicing the province from east to west and draining into the Aegean Sea. Fertile river valleys and a mountainous interior combined to form a pleasant land, with a strong, mixed economy and a large, relatively prosperous population. Many influential Greek cities were sprinkled throughout Asia, and three—Ephesus, Pergamum and Smyrna—held the official title "First of Asia." Of these, the primary city was the capital Ephesus, and it was from here that the gospel spread throughout the entire province, "among both Jews and Greeks" (Acts 19:10). Intensive missionary activity by the Apostles Paul and John, among others, resulted in a strong Christian presence throughout Asia by the late first century A.D. (note the "seven churches" of Revelation 1–3).

The temple of Hephaistos, the Agora at Athens, Greece.

Macedonia. The rugged, mountainous land of Macedonia sat astride the southern Balkan Peninsula just north of Achaia (Greece). Except for its southeastern exposure to the Aegean, Macedonia was not particularly oriented toward the sea. Because of its physical connection to the Balkans, growing conditions were affected more by the harsher climate of eastern Europe than that of the Mediterranean, and livestock and grains rather than grapes, olives and figs, provided its agricultural base. The entire ancient history of Macedonia was a history of conflict—both military and cultural—between the Macedonian and Greek populations of the lower Balkan Peninsula. Macedonia was the launching pad for the conquests of Alexander the Great, a native of that land who united the peninsula and then the known world under a blended, though predominantly Greek, culture known as Hellenism. Setting the stage for the New Testament, Caesar Augustus formally separated Macedonia from Achaia in 27 B.C. (cf. Acts 19:21), its more prominent and refined rival to the south. Two of Macedonia's main cities, Thessalonica and Philippi, figured prominently in the journeys of the Apostle Paul (Acts 16:9–12, 18:5), who founded important Christian churches among the Greek and Jewish populations of the region.

Achaia (Greece). Originally a small land lying just north of the Corinthian Gulf, Achaia by Roman times was enlarged to include the whole of Greece, including over two hundred islands scattered throughout the Aegean Sea. Achaia's most prominent region was the Peloponnesus, a tumbled peninsula shaped something like a mulberry leaf dangling into the Mediterranean by the narrow Isthmus of Corinth. The highly irregular coastline of Achaia brought the sea close to the land's dissected interior, providing vistas and venues that came to characterize the entire Greco-Roman world. With a mild climate but little in the way of natural resources, Achaia's prominence and wealth was found in its control of the shipping lanes of the eastern Mediterranean. City-states such as Athens, Corinth and Sparta, which for centuries had been fierce rivals for the body and mind of ancient Greece, were brought together into the Roman Empire in the second century B.C., while continuing to clamor for attention and privilege from Rome. The Apostle Paul was eagerly drawn into this challenging world and visited a number of Achaean cities on his second and third missionary journeys, focusing his work in particular in Athens and Corinth (Acts 17:16, 18:27–28; 2 Cor 1:1).

Crete. The large island of Crete, forming the southern boundary of the Aegean Sea, is strategically positioned as a bridge between the lands of the eastern and central Mediterranean basin. During the third and second millennia B.C. Crete was home to the pre-Greek Minoan civilization, but with the Minoan collapse the island lay awash a vast movement of peoples and cultures. Crete can probably be identified with biblical Caphtor, original homeland of the Philistines (Amos 9:7). Though always tied to the Greek mainland historically, Crete became a separate Roman province in 67 B.C. when, instead, it was joined administratively to Cyrene on the north African coast. In the first century A.D. Crete, like Achaia, boasted a large Greek population with a significant Jewish minority (Acts 2:11), but unlike the inhabitants of the classical mainland, Cretans had a low reputation in the ancient world (Titus 1:12, quoting the Cretan poet Epimenides). Crete is almost entirely covered with high mountains which were heavily forested in ancient times, and has only a few areas suitable for agriculture. The best harbors are on the northern shore. Paul's Rome-bound ship was unable to find suitable a winter harbor at Fair Havens, a rocky inlet midway along Crete's southern side where the island's mountains typically rise right out of the sea (Acts 27:8–13). Paul sent Titus to Crete to guide the growing churches there (Titus 1:5).

Illyricum. The Roman province of Illyricum lay along the eastern coast of the Adriatic Sea, from today's Albania to Croatia. With a cold, mountainous interior and a warm, inviting coast, the people of this region looked historically as much to Europe as to the Mediterranean. The region of Illyricum had been colonized as early as the eighth century B.C. by the Greeks yet lay largely outside of effective Greek control, and it harbored elements renowned for piracy on the Adriatic. Rome conquered the region in the mid-second century B.C., but the unrepressed nature of its inhabitants slowed full incorporation of the province into the Roman Empire until the first century A.D. The Romans divided the province of Illyricum into two major administrative sections; the more important of the two, Dalmatia, was visited by Titus (2 Tim 4:10). Illyricum's remoteness from the eastern Mediterranean world represents the far-flung distance that Paul traveled to preach the gospel (Rom 15:19). The extent of a Jewish presence there is unknown.

Italia (Rome). The boot-shaped Italian peninsula—probably the most distinctive coastline in the world—slices through the central Mediterranean Sea perfectly positioned to control the entire Mediterranean basin. The towering Alps have isolated the peninsula from mainland Europe, while the irregular, 3,220-kilometer (2000-mile) coastline provided ample harbors, especially in the southwest, to confirm Italy's destiny as a sea power from the beginning of its history. The Apennines, running the spine of the peninsula, are not particularly high mountains and did not provide a barrier to unification in antiquity. The mixture of climate, soil and water is good, blessing the inhabitants of the peninsula with the basic necessities of life. The magnificent city of Rome, straddling the Tiber, the only navigable river in the central peninsula, became synonymous with the vast empire that filled the Mediterranean basin by the first century B.C., washing ashore in Judea in the year 63. The adage "all roads lead to Rome" properly notes the intricate imperial highway system that was still expanding in the first century, although most transport always moved by sea. Mediterranean ports controlled by Rome were, by definition, the chief cities of the known world. A notable Jewish and emerging Christian presence was counted among Rome's cosmopolitan population in the first century A.D., and when Paul finally reached that city (Acts 27:1, 28:16) he was able to foster the growth of what was to become the most influential church in Christendom (Rom 1:7; cf. Heb 13:24).

Cyrenaica. The land of Cyrenaica stretched along a great bend of the north African coastline west of the Nile Delta, comprising a portion of both ancient and modern Libya. Because Cyrenaica backed up against the wasteland of the vast Saharan Desert, the attention of its inhabitants was directed toward the Mediterranean. This was a fertile land, and its excellent soil and pleasant climate combined to give the region a reputation known for bountiful grain fields and strong livestock. The region's main city, Cyrene, was founded by Greek colonists by the early sixth century B.C., only to be incorporated into Ptolemaic Egypt three hundred years later. It was under Ptolemaic rule that Cyrene became a renowned center of learning and medicine. The Romans officially joined the region to Crete in 67 B.C., uniting both lands into a single province named Cyrenaica, governed from Cyrene, the provincial capital. A large Jewish population had taken root in Cyrene during Ptolemaic times. During the first century A.D. the Jews of Cyrene maintained close ties to Jerusalem (Mt 27:32; Acts 2:10, 6:9), many no doubt coming into contact with the Gospel there. Christians from Cyrene helped to foster the growth of the early church in Antioch (Acts 11:20, 13:1).

Egypt. Perhaps no land in the ancient or classical world was better defined by its natural resources than was Egypt, the "Gift of the Nile." The immensely fertile Nile River valley, replenished each year by a new layer of rich flood-deposited silt, was only 10 to 26 kilometers (6 to 16 miles) wide, yet provided a steady crop of grain and vegetables to feed large portions of the Roman world. In the late second millennium B.C. Egypt was the strongest empire on earth, but its fortunes spiraled downward throughout the time of the Israelite monarchy. Ptolemaic Egypt (late fourth through first centuries B.C.) saw a meek attempt to revive past Egyptian glory, with Egyptian-based control extending over Cyrenecia and Syro-Palestine. With the suicide of Cleopatra VII (*the* Cleopatra) in 30 B.C., the last vestige of Pharaonic Egypt passed to Roman rule. Important Jewish colonies had been founded at Elephantine (Aswan), and especially in Alexandria on the Mediterranean coast, where Jews enjoyed a certain measure of autonomy. During the time of the New Testament, Alexandria was the greatest center of commerce and learning in the eastern Mediterranean, and Jews played an important role in both activities. This was fertile ground for Christianity as well, and the early Church took deep root in Egyptian soil (Acts 2:10, 18:24–28).

Arabia Petraea. The Arabia of the New Testament world consisted of a thin band of high rocky desert in what is today eastern and southern Jordan (including the ancient homelands of Moab and Edom) and the southern Sinai. This was the geographical and cultural seam between the peoples and lands of the eastern Mediterranean and those of the Arabian Peninsula. Traditionally home to a number of fiercely independent desert tribes, this region became dominated in the centuries leading up to the New Testament by the Nabateans. From their fabulous and fabled capital city of Petra, carved out of the red sandstone cliffs above the Rift Valley, the Nabateans dominated the great spice route that brought frankincense and myrrh from the recesses of the Arabian Peninsula into an eager Roman world. Nabatean control under Aretas IV, father-in-law of Herod Antipas, extended as far north as Damascus (2 Cor 11:32–33), and it was into this territory that the Apostle Paul retreated after becoming a follower of Jesus (Gal 1:17). When the Romans under Trajan were finally able to seize the Nabatean-held lands in A.D. 106, Arabia Petraea became the Empire's southeastern frontier.

The Intertestamental Period

Alexander the Great. Alexander of Macedon launched his campaign to conquer an aging Persian Empire in 334 B.C. Fearless and dynamic, the 20-year-old Alexander rode the rising tide of Hellenism, an equally vibrant way of life that would forever change the world. After sweeping through Asia Minor in just one year, Alexander fought his first major battle at Issus on the Cilician Plain, where the daring general routed the Persian king Darius. While Darius fled east, Alexander turned south, conquering Tyre in 332 B.C. after a seven-month siege and then easily subduing the remaining petty city-states that hugged the eastern Mediterranean seaboard. After being crowned Pharaoh in Egypt, Alexander retraced his steps up the eastern seaboard of the Mediterranean before catching up with Darius at Gaugamela in northern Mesopotamia. Here was the decisive battle, and after his ringing victory Alexander faced little real

Alexander the Great (left) from a mosaic found at Pompeii.

resistance as he marched all the way to the Indus Valley and the steppes of Central Asia. When he died at the age of 32 in Babylon, the seeds of a new world order had been sown across the entire ancient Near East. Alexander's soldiers settled down in his wake, establishing Macedonian colonies and cities throughout the former Persian Empire, including one in Samaria.

The Successors to Alexander. Upon his death, the fruit of Alexander's conquests passed to his generals. After two initial decades of war during which each general sought to gain advantage over the others, the world from Greece to Persia fell into an uneasy peace. The land of Palestine, including the Phoenician coast and Transjordan, came under the control of the Ptolemies, a long line of successors of Alexander's general Ptolemy who ruled from Egypt. The lands from Damascus to the Indus River were ruled by Seleucus, another of Alexander's generals, and his successors, most of whom were named Seleucus or Antiochus. The Seleucid kings in particular encouraged a policy of establishing a series of military colonies and Greek cities—many named Seleucia or Antioch—throughout the territory under their control. These served several purposes: to bind together an otherwise diverse and divisive land, to foster loyalty to the king, and to disseminate Hellenism among the native populations of the empire. During the third century B.C., Greek language and customs took deep root in Seleucid soil, finding life among many people—including Jews—who were attracted to new economic and cultural opportunities now available to them.

At the same time, the lands bordering the eastern seaboard of

THE ROUTE OF ALEXANDER THE GREAT, 334–323 B.C.

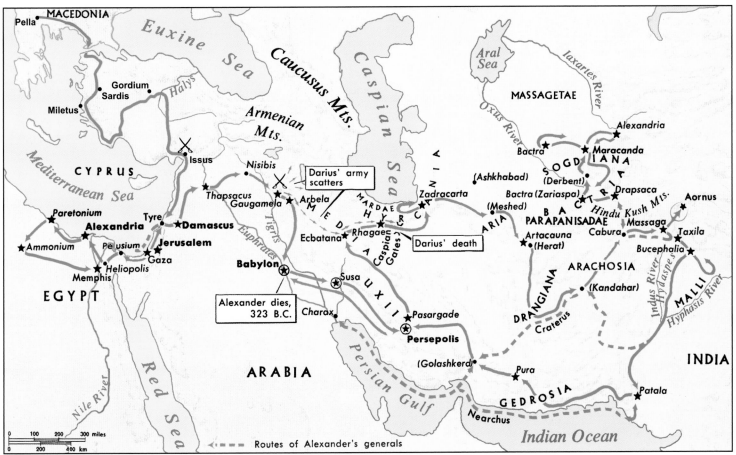

© Carta, Jerusalem

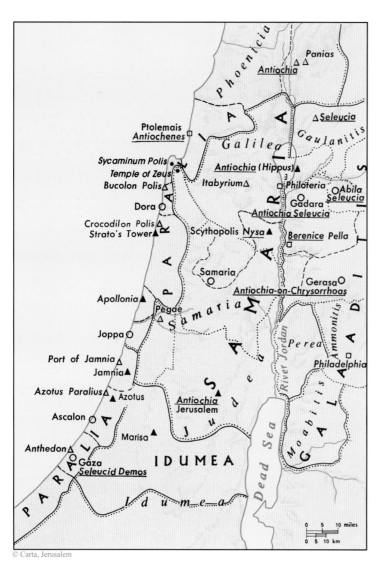

Seleucid war elephant.   *Seleucid coin with Apollo on reverse.*

———	Border of Seleucid eparchy
– – – –	Border of Ptolemaic city
··········	Border of Ptolemaic hyparchy
PARALIA	Seleucid eparchy
Judea	Ptolemaic hyparchy
Seleucia	City given Seleucid dynastic name
□	City given Ptolemaic dynastic name
○	City with municipal rights under Ptolemaic rule
△	Town given Greek name
▲	City given Greek name

© Carta, Jerusalem

the Mediterranean were buffeted by five Syrian wars as Seleucids fought Ptolemies for dominance over the region. With the Battle of Panias in 201 B.C., the border of Seleucid control was finally pushed south to Gaza. The Jews of Jerusalem welcomed the Seleucid king Antiochus III, who granted them rights and privileges that allowed relatively free expression of Jewish religious practices. Ominously, within a decade Antiochus III lost his holdings in Asia Minor to Rome, an emerging world power already poised to sweep into the lands of the Eastern Mediterranean.

The Maccabean Revolt. Antiochus IV took the Seleucid throne in 174 B.C. as Roman war clouds gathered on the western horizon. To meet this rising threat, Antiochus sought to strengthen his own far-flung empire by uniting its diverse lands and peoples under the religious and cultural flag of Hellenism, integrating all gods under the supremacy of Zeus. Certain elements among the population of Jerusalem accepted these decrees, while most, of course, resisted. At the highest levels, the office of the high priesthood was "purchased" by Jason, an ardent hellenizer, and then by Menelaus (2 Macc 4), two powerful men who tried to use their position to bend the cultural and religious loyalty of the Jews toward Hellenism. When Antiochus IV invaded Egypt to try to forge a single political unit out of all of the eastern lands, Rome stepped in. Humiliated and frustrated on the world stage, Antiochus turned his wrath against the Jewish population of Jerusalem, who had largely rebuffed his earlier attempts to hellenize their city and bring it into his cultural and political fold. Antiochus forbade the exercise of religious practices essential to Judaism (such as keeping the Sabbath and yearly feasts, offering

sacrifices and circumcision) and in December 167 B.C. he turned the Temple into a sanctuary of Zeus, offering on its altar sacrifices unclean according to Jewish law (1 Macc 1:41–64).

With this the Jews mounted an armed revolt, prompted by Mattathias, a priest of the Hasmonean family who hailed from the village of Modiin, located on the edge of Palestine's hellenized coastal plain. Mattathias's son Judas Maccabeus ("the hammerer") waged what amounted to a guerrilla war against the Seleucid army, which was trying to link with the Hellenistic forces in Jerusalem and crush the Jewish revolt. A brilliant battle tactician, Judas routed the Seleucid forces at each attempt, finally taking his own army into Jerusalem. In December 164 B.C. Judas cleansed and rededicated the Temple (1 Macc 2–4); the festival of Hanukkah ("Dedication"; cf. Jn 10: 22–23) commemorates this event.

Not content with rescuing the Temple from Seleucid hands, Judas launched a series of defensive campaigns aimed at strengthening the Jewish position in their historic homeland. Judas himself fell in battle in 161 B.C., but over the next two decades his brothers Jonathan and Simon gained decisive victories over the Seleucids in Samaria, Galilee, Transjordan (Gilead and Syria) and even the coastal plain, long a stronghold of Greek culture and power (1 Macc 10–15). The Seleucid king formally recognized Judea's independence under Simon in 142 B.C. (1 Macc 13:33–42), signaling the rise of the first independent Jewish state since the fall of Judah to the Babylonians in 586 B.C. In response, the Jews granted Simon the title "leader and high priest forever, until a trustworthy prophet should arise" (1 Macc 14:25–49).

The Hasmonean State. With its newly won political and religious independence in hand, the Jewish state began to consolidate and expand power in its ancestral homeland. John Hyrcanus succeeded his father Simon in 135 B.C. and, with the tacit approval of Rome, formally conquered Medeba in Transjordan, Samaria (where he destroyed the Samaritan temple on Mount Gerizim) and Idumea, thereby securing for Judea the lands which were best placed strategically for later territorial expansion. Toward the end of his reign Hyrcanus sided with the Sadducees over against the Pharisees in inter-Jewish religious affairs, signaling a gradual shift toward hellenization within the ruling administration of Judea (as the party of the wealthy Jewish aristocracy, the Sadducees were more in touch with the social and economic opportunities that arose with Hellenism than were the more conservative Pharisees). That Hyrcanus gave his sons (and successors) Greek names (Aristobulus and Alexander Janneus) is a further indication of the inter-Jewish religious and cultural strife that lay ahead.

Hyrcanus was succeeded by his older son Aristobulus in 104 B.C. During his one-year reign Aristobulus was able to conquer Galilee, reportedly forcing its inhabitants to be circumcised. His successor, Alexander Janneus, pushed the borders of the Hasmonean kingdom to their greatest extent, to include essentially the same territory that had been controlled by David and Solomon. Of particular importance was the conquest of all of the Greek cities on the coastal plain (except Ascalon). In internal affairs, however, the Judean king was less successful. Janneus's favor for things Hellenistic, combined with gross personal moral failings, brought him into open conflict with the Pharisees, who represented the conservative masses of the population. Janneus suppressed the Pharisees with cruel force, at one time crucifying 800 of them.

Janneus's queen, Salome Alexandra, succeeded him as ruler in 76 B.C. Her largely peaceful reign was marred by conflict between her two sons and heirs-apparent, Hyrcanus II (favored by both the Pharisees and the queen) to whom she granted the high priesthood, and Aristobulus II (favored by the Sadducees) who controlled the army. Upon her death in 67 B.C., the brothers waged civil war. Both Hyrcanus II and Aristobulus II asked Rome to intervene on their behalf. Rome was all too happy to oblige; using the chaos of the time as an excuse, the army of Pompey entered Jerusalem in 63 B.C. and the Hasmonean kingdom came to an ignoble end.

Herod the Great. Pompey reorganized the lands of the now defunct Hasmonean kingdom in order to incorporate its territory into the fold of the Roman Empire. Greek cities occupied by the Jews since the days of Hyrcanus—those on the coastal plain, Sebaste in Samaria, Scythopolis and various cities in Transjordan, together with their agricultural hinterlands—were made into autonomous units under the supervision of the Roman proconsul in Syria. The Transjordanian cities were then joined into a league called the Decapolis, filling a territory strategically located to guard Rome's eastern frontier against its political and cultural foes. The Jews retained areas most densely settled by them: Judea, a large portion of Galilee and, across the Jordan, Perea. Hyrcanus II was appointed as high priest over this shell of his former kingdom, but administrative control was given to Antipater the Idumean, who had acted as the behind-the-scenes power broker during the last years of Hasmonean rule. Antipater appointed his older son Phasael governor of Jerusalem and his younger son, Herod, as governor of Galilee.

For two decades various factions vied for control of the land, some struggling to revive the forces of Jewish nationalism, others opting for a form of Roman supremacy. Throughout, Herod maintained a firm, if ruthless, grip on Galilee. This struggle grew to

Judea at the beginning of the revolt
Additions of Jonathan, 160–142 B.C.
Additions of Simon, 142–134 B.C.
Additions of Hyrcanus I, 134–104 B.C.
Additions of Aristobulus I, 104–103 B.C.
Additions of Alexander Janneus 103–76 B.C.
Kingdom of Alexander Janneus

0   10 mi.
0   15 km

© Carta, Jerusalem

a climax with the murder of Antipater in 43 B.C. and the invasion of Jerusalem by the Parthians three years later. The Parthians, who controlled Mesopotamia, were Rome's greatest enemy to the East. The Jews who remained in Mesopotamia after the Babylonian Exile represented an important minority population within Parthian controlled lands. They supported the Parthian invasion of Jerusalem as a means of reestablishing an independent Jewish state in Judea. Herod, facing his match, fled to Rome where the Senate responded by appointing him king of all Judea. Eager to reclaim his throne, Herod landed his army at Ptolemais, the port of Galilee, in 39 B.C., then embarked on a series of ferocious campaigns against forces loyal to the Hasmoneans. Within two years he had subdued the land, emerging as the sole, undisputed and largely unloved ruler of Judea. Certain territorial additions on the coast and in Transjordan were added over the next couple of decades, giving Herod a territory, with some modifications in northern Transjordan, reminiscent of that of Alexander Janneus.

A megalomaniac by nature, Herod was restrained from further territorial expansion by Caesar Augustus. Instead, he directed his enormous energies inward, in a personal building campaign that was unsurpassed in the ancient world. Each of his projects, including Jerusalem's Temple Mount, was built in an architectural style that proclaimed the glorious presence of Rome.

- Herod's most prominent building projects were in **Jerusalem**. Here Herod built for himself a sumptuous palace in the north-

Legend:
- ★ Military colony founded by Herod
- ⊙ Herodian fortress
- ▒ Herod's kingdom at the start of his reign
- ░ Additions to Herod's kingdom

© Carta, Jerusalem

Coin of Herod the Great.

western corner of the Upper City (the area of today's Jaffa Gate), guarded by three massive towers. The Temple Mount was doubled in size and encircled by a massive portico. The Temple itself was rebuilt entirely, and the Antonia Fortress constructed to overshadow the Temple Mount from the north. Herod also built a theater and a stadium in the city, and strengthened its fortifications.

- Herod founded **Caesarea** (cf. Acts 8:40, 10:1, 18:22, 21:8), a new port city on the Sharon Plain, to provide better sea access to both Judea and Galilee. Well planned and developed, the city boasted a theater and an amphitheater, a magnificent palace on the sea, a temple dedicated to Caesar, an aqueduct and, most importantly, a harbor projecting far into the Mediterranean that was held together by underwater mortar.

- Herod built a number of palace fortresses in the rugged wilderness east and southeast of Jerusalem, both to secure his back flank into Judea and to provide places of refuge during times of unrest. These included **Herodium**, **Hyrcania**, **Alexandrium**, **Cypros**, **Masada** and, east of the Dead Sea, **Machaerus**. Some of these fortresses had previously served the Hasmonean kings. At Masada Herod especially expressed his grandeur, bring-

ing all the comforts of Rome to an otherwise totally inhospitable corner of his kingdom.

- Herod also rebuilt and enlarged the old Hasmonean palace complex at the oasis of **Jericho**. Here he could escape the winter chill of Jerusalem and banquet in decadent splendor amid pools, fountains, baths, gardens and columned courtyards. The opulence of Herod's Jericho attracted both rich opportunists (cf. Lk 19:1–8) and the desperately poor (cf. Lk 18:35–43).

- Caesar Augustus granted to Herod the city of Samaria (cf. Acts 8:5, 15:3), a bastion of Hellenism since the days of Alexander, and in gratitude Herod renamed the city **Sebaste** (Greek for Augustus). Herod refortified the site, settled foreign mercenaries there and built a temple to Caesar Augustus so colossal that it could be seen by ships on the Mediterranean.

- Augustus also gave Herod the region northeast of Galilee that included the springs of the Jordan River. The easternmost spring was already a center of worship for the Greco-Roman god Pan, and it was here that Herod built a temple faced with white marble, also dedicated to Augustus. In 2 B.C. Herod's son Philip renamed the site **Caesarea Philippi** (cf. Mt 16:13).

Map

Legend:
- Territory under Philip
- Territory under Antipas
- Territory under the Procurator of Judea
- Territory under the Proconsul of Syria

Sidon
Damascus
Tyre
TYRE
ULATHA
Caesarea Philippi
Thella
Raphana
Gischala
UPPER GALILEE
GAULANITIS
BATANEA
TRACHONITIS
Ptolemais (Acco)
Baca
Bersabe
Kefar Hananiya
Gabara
Chabulon
LOWER GALILEE
Jotapata
Taricheae
Canatha
Sepphoris
Tiberias
Hippus
Dion
AURANITIS
Nazareth
Abila
Dora
Japhia
Gadara
Edrei
Mediterranean Sea
Esdraelon Valley
DECAPOLIS
Scythopolis
Bostra
Caesarea
Pella
Sebaste
Mt. Gerizim
Amathus
Gerasa
Apollonia
SAMARIA
PEREA
Antipatris
Joppa
Lydda
Archelais
Gadora
J U D E A
Neara
Philadelphia
Jamnia
Emmaus (Nicopolis)
Abila
Jericho
Jerusalem
Beth-ramatha
Azotus
Ascalon
I D U M E A
Machaerus
Gaza
Hebron
Dead Sea
Masada
Beersheba
NABATEANS

0 10 mi.
0 15 km

© Carta, Jerusalem

Site of Caesarea Philippi (modern Banias).

Through these building projects, Herod sought to appease his insatiable ego, to secure his rule, to provide his people with work and to entice their loyalty and devotion to him.

The end of Herod's reign was filled with civil and domestic unrest, much of it fostered by his own family as various sons fought to inherit the throne. Into this volatile fray came Magi from the East (probably from Parthia, Herod's old nemesis who had already driven him from Judea once, at the beginning of his reign), looking for the legitimate king of the Jews (Mt 2:1–12). Herod's response to kill the babies of Bethlehem was overreaching, yet true to form.

Upon Herod's death in 4 B.C., Augustus divided the kingdom between Herod's three surviving sons. Archelaus was appointed ethnarch over Judea, Idumea and Samaria. Herod Antipas was given two primarily Jewish areas, Galilee and Perea. Herod Philip received lands in northern Transjordan including Gaulanitis, where relatively new Jewish settlers mixed with a deeply rooted Hellenistic population. Antipas and Philip stayed in office throughout the lifetime of Jesus (cf. Lk 3:1, 3:19). In contrast, Rome banished Archelaus (Mt 2:22) to Gaul in A.D. 6 for gross incompetence, preferring instead to rule Judea through a string of procurators such as Pontius Pilate (A.D. 26–36; cf. Lk 3:1).

Jewish Religious and Political Parties at the Time of the New Testament. In the first century Judaism was multi-faceted and sectarian, with various parties competing for the allegiance of the people of Judea. Of these, Josephus mentions four groups: Pharisees, Sadducees, Essenes and a "fourth philosophy" which was probably the Zealots. Although their origins are lost in time, by the time of the New Testament these parties were deeply rooted in the old clash between Jewish nationalism and religion on the one hand and various forces of Hellenism—including the occupying might of imperial Rome—on the other.

- **Pharisees**. The Pharisees—about 6,000 in number—were the leading Jewish party in Jesus' day and held great influence over the general populace. Like the scribes, the Pharisees were scholar-teachers and could be found scattered among the towns and villages of Judea and Galilee, wherever there was a Jewish community large enough to support a synagogue. Pharisaic authority was grounded in a scrupulous adherence to the Oral Law, the Torah-based "tradition of the elders" which had been handed down faithfully since the time of Moses. The Pharisees maintained a system of strict religious practices, holding others accountable for not adhering to the same. Opposed to the forces of Hellenism, the Pharisees were also champions of Jewish political freedom. Jesus' teachings were more closely aligned to the Pharisees than to any other religious party (Mt 23:2–3), and the Apostle Paul was trained as a Pharisee (Phil 3:5–6).

- **Sadducees**. Though smaller in number than the Pharisees, the Sadducees exerted greater influence at the higher levels of religion and politics since they represented the Jewish urban, landed aristocracy. Based in Jerusalem, the Sadducees controlled the high priesthood and other influential positions in the

Early Caesars of the Roman Empire

Caesar	Years of Reign	New Testament References	Selected Notes of New Testament Significance
Julius Caesar	49–44 B.C.	—	—
Second Triumvirate (Mark Antony, Octavian, Lepidus)	44–31 B.C.	—	—
Augustus (Octavian)	31 (27) B.C.–A.D. 14	Luke 2:1	Patron of Herod the Great; Caesar at Jesus' birth
Tiberius	A.D. 14–37	Matthew 22:17, 22:21; Luke 3:1, 23:2; John 19:12, 19:15	Caesar during Jesus' ministry; namesake of Herod Antipas' capital on the Sea of Galilee
Caligula (Gaius)	A.D. 37–41	—	—
Claudius	A.D. 41–54	Acts 11:28, 17:7, 18:2	Caesar during Paul's first two missionary journeys
Nero	A.D. 54–68	Acts 25:11–12, 26:32, 27:24, 28:19; Phil 4:22	Caesar during Paul's third missionary journey and Roman imprisonment; executed Paul and Peter
Galba, Otho and Vitellius ("the year of the three emperors")	A.D. 68–69	—	—
Vespasian	A.D. 69–79	—	As general, led Roman forces against the Jewish Revolt in A.D. 66–69
Titus	A.D. 79–81	—	As general, defeated Judea and destroyed Jerusalem in A.D. 70
Domitian	A.D. 81–96	—	Caesar during John's exile in Patmos; great persecution of the church
Nerva	A.D. 96–98	—	—
Trajan	A.D. 98–117	—	Annexed the Nabatean realms in A.D. 106
Hadrian	A.D. 117–130	—	Suppressed the Second Jewish (Bar Kochba) Revolt

The Herods

Name	Relationship to Herod the Great	Greatest Extent of Territory Ruled	Title and Dates of Reign	New Testament References
Antipater I	Grandfather of Herod the Great	Idumea	Governor during the reign of Alexander Jannaeus	—
Antipater II	Father of Herod the Great	Greater Judea (including Idumea, Samaria, Galilee and Perea)	*De facto* administrator from 63–55 B.C.; procurator from 55–43 B.C.	—
Herod I (the Great)	—	Greater Judea (including Idumea, Samaria, Galilee, Perea, Gaulanitis and surrounding regions)	King from 37–4 B.C.	Mt 2:1–22; Lk 1:5
Archelaus	Oldest son of Herod the Great	Judea, Samaria and Idumea	Ethnarch from 4 B.C.–A.D. 6	Mt 2:22
Herod Philip	Son of Herod the Great	Gaulanitis and surrounding regions	Tetrarch from 4 B.C.–A.D. 34	Lk 3:1
Herod Antipas	Son of Herod the Great	Galilee and Perea	Tetrarch from 4 B.C.–A.D. 39	Mt 14:1–11; Mk 6:14–29; Lk 3:1, 3:19, 13:31–33, 23:7–12
Herod Agrippa I	Grandson of Herod the Great	Greater Judea (same land as ruled by Herod the Great)	King from A.D. 37–44	Acts 12:1, 12:18–23
Herod Agrippa II	Great grandson of Herod the Great	Chalcis (southeastern Lebanon); Gaulanitis and surrounding regions; parts of Galilee and Perea	King of Chalcis from A.D. 48–53; Tetrarch of Gaulanitis and surrounding regions and parts of Galilee and Perea from A.D. 53–c. 100	Acts 25:13–26:32

Remains of the Essene settlement of Qumran, looking east toward the Dead Sea and the mountains of Moab.

government of Jewish affairs. The Sadducees were generally wealthy, well-educated, and eager to advance their standing through contacts with the outside world, all characteristics that tended to separate them from the masses. As a whole, the Sadducees sought to build a Hellenistic state on a Jewish national foundation, a combination that was rejected by most Jews in Jesus' day.

- **Essenes**. About 4,000 in number, the Essenes devoted themselves to an aesthetic, monastic lifestyle emphasizing ritual purity, communal meals, study and prayer. Viewing the high priesthood and Jerusalem Temple worship as corrupt, the Essenes withdrew, under the leadership of the Teacher of Righteousness, from normative Jewish society to await the dramatic, foreordained intervention of God on their behalf at the end of time. The Essenes looked to the coming of two Messiahs, a priestly Messiah "from Aaron" who would redeem Temple worship and a royal Messiah "from Israel" who would restore the Davidic line. Most Essenes lived communally in and around the settlement of Qumran on the northwestern shore of the Dead Sea; their writings, the Dead Sea Scrolls, are an important window into their own community as well as into the world of the Gospels. There is evidence that some Essenes also lived in Jerusalem and other towns and villages in Judea.

- **Zealots**. The term "Zealot"—reflecting more a way of thought than a formal party—encompassed a number of independent groups whose overall goals were to restore political independence to Judea and to improve the socioeconomic plight of the masses. Toward this end, Zealot bands attracted persons who not only squirmed under the heavy hand of Rome, but also suffered injustices perpetrated by wealthy and powerful Jews, especially by Jews who collaborated with the Romans. Galilee in particular was a fertile breeding ground for nationalistic movements due largely to its position as an open Jewish frontier, and during the first century A.D. several messiah figures arose from Galilee to try to overthrow Roman rule in the land (cf. Acts 5:37). The last defenders of Masada were Zealots, let by the Galilean Eleazar.

Jesus counted a Zealot among his twelve disciples (Mk 3:18).

The vast majority of first-century Jews, however, did not formally belong to any of these parties—they were simply *am haaretz*, "people of the land." This multitude, largely composed of lower class peasants—regular folks just trying to get by—often felt alienated in their own land (cf. Jn 7:49). Not particularly well-educated and suffering under a tax burden estimated to be between 50 and 70 percent of personal income, the multitudes simply wanted to live quiet and secure lives, much like people do everywhere. Caught between the "traditions of the fathers" and new ways of the world, these were people who sought the ways of God amidst the challenges of everyday life.

> And so Jesus went about all the cities and the villages, teaching in their synagogues and proclaiming the gospel of the kingdom, and healing every kind of disease and every kind of sickness. Seeing the multitudes, He felt compassion for them, because they were distressed and downcast like sheep without a shepherd.
>
> (Mt 9:35–36)

The Gospels

The Birth and Early Years of Jesus. The Gospel story opens with Luke's account of the births of John the Baptist and Jesus in the last days of the tumultuous reign of Herod the Great (Lk 1–2). John was born into a priestly family which, according to tradition, lived in Ein Kerem, a small village nestled in the rugged hills just west of Jerusalem. Mary, a poor peasant girl from the Galilean village of Nazareth, three-days' journey to the north, visited John's mother Elizabeth while she herself was pregnant with Jesus. She returned to the region some months later with Joseph, giving birth to Jesus in the city of David, Bethlehem of Judea, Joseph's ancestral home. Geographically, Bethlehem lay equidistant between Herodium—Herod's desert fortress representing the intrusive world of Rome—and Jerusalem, the world center of Judaism. Lying in the shadow of both and rooted in the royal line of David, Bethlehem was a fitting birthplace for a baby destined to usher in the Kingdom of God.

Jesus' first visitors were simple shepherds from nearby fields (Lk 2:8); that they were tending their flocks on ground that would normally be sown with grain between November and April suggests that the Christmas story probably took place in the summertime, when Judean sheep and goats typically grazed on field stubble. The subsequent visit to Bethlehem of Magi "from the east" (Mt 2:1–12) indicates that, like Solomon (cf. 1 Kgs 9:26–10:29; cf. Isa 60:6), Jesus was a king worthy of receiving the tribute of the world. The Magi's gifts—gold, frankincense and myrrh—were typical of the commodities entering the Roman world through Palestine via the Nabatean-controlled Arabian spice route.

Mary, Joseph and Jesus subsequently fled to Egypt to escape the wrath of Herod (Mt 2:13–18), no doubt finding shelter among the large Jewish population there. Coptic tradition identifies several sites visited by the Holy Family while in Egypt. Sometime after the death of Herod in 4 B.C. Joseph took his family back to Judea, then on to Nazareth in Galilee, preferring to live under the rule of Herod's more even-handed son Antipas rather than in a Judea controlled by Archelaus, a king who had inherited much of his father's temperament (Mt 2:19–23).

Joseph settled in Nazareth, a small, nondescript village in a chalky basin high atop a limestone ridge that overlooks the Jezreel Valley from the north. Nazareth was a village largely lacking in economic opportunities (Mt 2:23; cf. Jn 1:46). Jesus, like all growing boys in the first century, learned his family trade, in this case the specialized skills of a "carpenter," a worker in wood and stone, the local building materials (cf. Mt 13:55). It is likely that jobs were scarce in Nazareth and therefore possible that both Joseph and Jesus honed their skills in Sepphoris, Galilee's capital city in the Beth Netofa Valley five miles north of Nazareth. Here jobs were plentiful, as the city was undergoing a massive rebuilding campaign financed by Herod Antipas.

Jesus was also raised in the Jewish "tradition of the elders" (cf. Lk 2:52). One might imagine that as a boy he often gazed into the vast Jezreel Valley from high atop the Nazareth Ridge, recalling to mind God's great redemptive acts of old that took place there, nearly at his doorstep—the battles of Deborah, Barak (Judg 4–5) and Gideon (Judg 6–8) and the ministries of Elijah (1 Kgs 17–19) and Elisha (2 Kgs 4–5). In addition, Gath-hepher, hometown of the prophet Jonah (2 Kgs 14:25; Jonah 1:1), was an hour's walk northeast of Nazareth. One might also suppose that Jesus' awareness of such Galilee connections helped to shape his resolve later in life. In the spring when he was twelve, Jesus traveled to Jerusalem with his parents to celebrate the Passover festival. He stayed behind when his parents began their return trip home; retracing their steps to Jerusalem, they found him in intense debate with teachers in the Temple (Lk 2:41–51).

Jesus' Baptism and Move to Capernaum. Based on data provided in the Gospels, it is not possible to establish a definitive chronology of Jesus' ministry, or to be certain of his travel itineraries or even the number of times that he visited Jerusalem. Jesus began his ministry when he was about thirty years old (Lk 3:23), and most interpreters reconstruct a three-year ministry based on the number of Passover festivals mentioned in the Gospel of John (2:13, 6:4, 11:55).

John the Baptist began preaching "a baptism of repentance for the forgiveness of sins" in the fifteenth year of Tiberius Caesar, A.D. 27–28 (Lk 3:1–3). John's activity was concentrated in the Jordan Valley, from the south at Bethabara (i.e., "Bethany beyond the Jordan"; Jn 1:28)—just a day's walk for the multitudes of Jerusalem (Mt 3:1–12; Lk 3:4–17)—to Aenon near Salim, east of Samaria (Jn 3:23). His bold message has been likened to those of both Elijah and the Essenes, and was part of the spiritual fervor that gripped Judea in his day. The beginning of Jesus' public ministry was marked by his baptism by John (Mt 3:13–17; Lk 3:21–22). Immediately afterward Jesus spent forty days in seclusion in the wilderness of Judea, probably in the empty hills above Jericho. Throughout history this desolate terrain has been a place of retreat and refuge, and it was here that Jesus successfully overcame the temptations of Satan (Lk 4:1–13). For his part, John eventually ran afoul of the authorities. He was arrested and beheaded by Herod Antipas—in Machaerus, according to Josephus—for criticizing Antipas's marriage to his brother Philip's wife (Mt 14:1–12; Lk 3:19–20).

The wilderness of Judea, above Jericho, where Jesus spent forty days in seclusion.

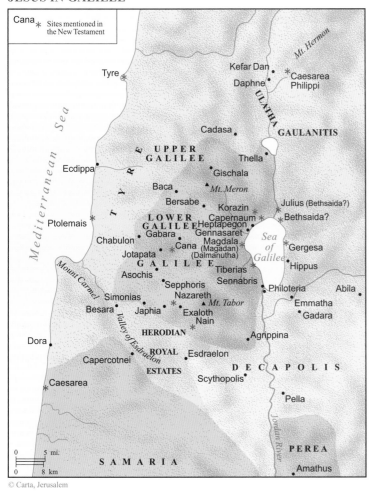

Map labels:
Cana * Sites mentioned in the New Testament

Tyre *
Kefar Dan
Daphne
Caesarea Philippi
Mt. Hermon
ULATHA
Cadasa
GAULANITIS
Ecdippa
UPPER GALILEE
Thella
Gischala
Baca
Mt. Meron
Bersabe
Korazin
Julius (Bethsaida?)
Ptolemais *
LOWER GALILEE
Capernaum
Heptapegon
Bethsaida?
Chabulon
Gabara
Gennasaret
Jotapata
Cana
Magdala (Magadan) (Dalmanutha)
Sea of Galilee
Gergesa
GALILEE
Tiberias
Hippus
Asochis
Sennabris
Sepphoris
Philoteria
Abila
Simonias
Nazareth
Besara
Japhia
Mt. Tabor
Emmatha
Exaloth
Gadara
Nain
Dora
HERODIAN
Agrippina
ROYAL ESTATES
Esdraelon
Capercotnei
Esdraelon
DECAPOLIS
Caesarea
Scythopolis
Pella
Mediterranean Sea
TYRE
Mount Carmel
Valley of Esdraelon
Jordan River
PEREA
SAMARIA
Amathus

0 5 mi.
0 8 km

© Carta, Jerusalem

Jesus' initial Galilean ministry appears to have been based in Nazareth, with travels taking him throughout the region to villages such as Cana and Capernaum. He soon attracted a significant crowd of followers, including members of his own family (Lk 4:14–15; Jn 2:12). The Gospels provide various accounts of Jesus' calling of his twelve disciples (Mt 4:18–22; Mk 1:16–20, 2:14, 3:13–19; Lk 5:1–11; Jn 1:19–51). Most of his disciples were from villages that bordered the northern shore of the Sea of Galilee such as Capernaum and Bethsaida, and several were fishermen. James and John, sons of Zebedee, probably stood to inherit a rather profitable fishing business (cf. Mk 1:20). Notable also were Matthew (Levi), a tax collector, and Simon the Zealot, Matthew's socio-economic rival. The name "Iscariot" may have indicated that Judas was the lone Judean of the group (from the village of Kirioth), or that he was a member of the radical Zealot group Sicarii ("assassins"). In any case, it is clear that together, Jesus' small band of disciples represented a cross section of the peoples of Galilee.

Jesus performed his first miracle at Cana, a village on the northern edge of the Beth Netofa Valley three hours' walk from Nazareth. Here, at a wedding, he turned water into wine (Jn 2:1–11), the first of several instances in which Jesus seemed to pattern his ministry after that of Elisha (Elisha's first miracle was to make bad water good; cf. 2 Kgs 2:19–22; Jesus' first miracle was to turn already good water better). On a later visit to Cana Jesus healed the son of a royal official, a man who was probably attached to the court of Herod Antipas (Jn 4:46–54).

Jesus steadily gained a following throughout Galilee, but had less success back home in Nazareth. There he met resistance in the local synagogue when he unfavorably compared his nationalistic townsfolk to the Sidonians and Syrians, Israel's cultural and political enemies during the days of Elijah and Elisha (Lk 4:16–30; cf. Mt 13:53–58). This was a particularly sensitive issue in Galilee, a Jewish frontier land bordering these regions. Escaping from Nazareth with his life, Jesus moved to Capernaum for good (Lk 4:31). The prophet Isaiah had known that because of its location, Galilee would always face the dark threat of invasion and so coined the phrase "Galilee of the *Gentiles*" (Isa 9:1). Citing Isaiah in this regard, Matthew notes that with Jesus' move from Nazareth to Capernaum, a light was now dawning on a land overshadowed by death (Mt 4:12–17).

Jesus' Galilean Ministry from Capernaum. It should not be supposed that Jesus' move to Capernaum was an attempt to withdraw from the limelight and spend quiet time along the shores of a gentle sea. Rather, in the first century A.D. three distinct political units bordered the Sea of Galilee. By focusing his ministry around this sea, Jesus was able to come into contact with people who represented the full scope of religious, social and political identities found in first-century Palestine.

- **Galilee** proper, on the west side of the Sea, was under the control of Herod Antipas. Galilee included towns such as Capernaum, Magdala and Tiberias (Jn 6:23), Herod Antipas's newly founded capital city (since A.D. 17). Galilee was primarily a Jewish region, with some corridors of Hellenism.
- **Gaulanitis**, rising from the northeast corner of the Sea, included Bethsaida and Caesarea Philippi. Governed by Herod Philip, Gaulanitis was an area of decidedly mixed Jewish-Hellenistic sentiments.
- The region of **Decapolis** touched the southeastern quarter of the Sea. This was an "in-your-face" bastion of Hellenism and Roman imperial might, established to guard Rome's eastern frontier.

In addition, geographical, archaeological and textual evidence suggest that Capernaum, Jesus' adopted hometown (Mt 9:1), was a bustling population center. The city lay astride the main highway linking Galilee's coast to Damascus. Capernaum was the last town in Galilee before reaching Gaulanitis, and so it was appropriate that there was a tax office alongside the road (cf. Mk 2:14). Moreover, with at least eight large stone piers—the most of any town on the Sea of Galilee in Jesus' days—Capernaum was a center of fishing and related industries (boat- and net-manufacture, fish processing and distribution). The outlying regions of Capernaum were devoted to agriculture, as was the case for every town and village in Galilee (cf. Mk 2:23, 4:1–9), but the city was also apparently a center for

Remains of the Late Roman period synagogue at Capernaum.

23

Modern Kursi (Gergesa), on the eastern shore of the Sea of Galilee.

manufacturing heavy food-processing equipment such as grain mills and olive presses. Finally, a Roman garrison was based in Capernaum; its commander fronted the money to build the town's synagogue (Lk 7:2–5). In all, it is certain that in Capernaum, Jesus faced the busyness and challenges of life no less than did his contemporaries. Occasionally, however, he withdrew in the early morning to "a lonely place" (Mk 1:35)—probably the rocky basalt hills above Capernaum—to gaze out over the awakening world of the Sea and pray in solitude.

Except for a few journeys, Jesus' entire ministry before his final departure to Jerusalem took place around the northern half of the Sea of Galilee (also called the Lake of Gennesaret—Lk 5:1; or the Sea of Tiberias—Jn 6:1, 21:1; cf. Mk 2:13, 4:1). Here, along pathways connecting villages, in homes and in fields, Jesus found numerous illustrations for his parables of the kingdom, stories with teaching points grounded in everyday life (e.g., Mt 5:13–16, 7:13–23, 12:1–7, 13:1–52; Lk 13–16). Large multitudes from the entire area seemed to follow his every move; most were Jewish (from Galilee, Judea, Jerusalem, Idumea and Perea—Mk 3:7–8), but others hailed from Gentile regions (the vicinity of Tyre and Sidon—Mk 3:8). Initially, Jesus' ministry focused on the "lost sheep of the house of Israel" (Mt 10:6), and so he sent his own disciples into the towns and villages of Jewish Galilee to preach, teach, heal (Mt 10:1–23; Mk 6:7–13) and, like him, to "go about doing good" (Acts 10:28). Eventually his ministry—and theirs—reached into Gentile areas as well.

Jesus performed most of his miracles in Capernaum, Bethsaida and Chorazin (Mt 11:20–24; cf. Lk 10:13–16), three towns forming a triangle on the northern shore of the Sea of Galilee. We can only surmise what most of these miracles may have been, since the Gospels mention only a very few in the vicinity of Bethsaida and none at all in Chorazim (cf. Jn 21:25).

The Gospels record several visits of Jesus to synagogues in Nazareth, Capernaum, Jerusalem and elsewhere (Mt 12:9, 13:54; Mk 1:21, 3:1; Lk 4:16; Jn 6:59, 18:20). We can assume that Jesus attended the synagogue every Sabbath, in whatever town or village that he happened to be in at the time. There is abundant literary evidence that many towns and villages throughout Judea, Galilee and the world of the Diaspora had synagogues during the time of the New Testament. Synagogues from the first century A.D. have

been found at Masada, Herodium and Gamala, and a recently excavated building at Jericho that was probably a synagogue dates to the first century B.C. The synagogue was the main public institution for Judaism, where the community met every Sabbath day and on holy days to read the Torah and *Haftorah* (prophetic writings), to pray and listen to sermons or homilies. Jesus was often invited to read from the Scriptures and deliver the sermon when he attended synagogue. He soon gained a reputation for teaching "with authority" (Mt 7:28–29; Mk 1:22), with the result that he often locked horns with the local religious establishment (e.g., Mt 21:23; Lk 4:16–30; Jn 9:22–23).

Jesus often traveled across the sea by boat and these journeys could end unpredictably, if, for instance, a powerful storm churned up the lake, a frequent occurrence during the winter months. While waves on the sea rarely exceed 1.5 meters (4 to 5 feet) in height in even the fiercest storms, Galilean fishing boats in the first century A.D. were not particularly large (the "Jesus boat" at Ginnosar, an Israeli kibbutz on the northwestern shore of the Sea of Galilee, measures 8 meters/27 feet in length) and could easily be swamped if heavily loaded. Such a storm caught Jesus' disciples off guard one evening as they were sailing from Capernaum to the other side of the lake, probably intending to land, as they often did, in the territory controlled by Herod Philip (Mk 4:35–41). Jesus, asleep in the stern, was awakened by his frantic disciples and promptly calmed the sea, rebuking the evil chaos that ancient Israel had long pictured as deep, churning waters (v. 39; cf. Gen 1:2; Ps 107:29; Jonah 1:4–16; Rev 21:1).

The boat reached shore in the country of the Gergasenes (Mt 8:28; Mk 5:1; some versions read Gadarenes or Gerasenes). While some scholars place the following event in the region of Gadara (a Decapolis city whose territory touched the southern end of the sea) or even in Gerasa (i.e., Jerash, another Decapolis city high in the Transjordanian hills), geographical logic suggests that the boat was blown into the harbor of Gergesa (modern Kursi), a small fishing village just on the Decapolis side of the border with Gaulanitis, Philip's territory. Here Jesus healed a wild, animal-like man possessed by demons, sending the demons into a large herd of pigs which promptly ran down a cliff and were drowned in the sea—returning to the chaos, as it were, from which they came (Mk 5:2–17). A rather steep hill drops directly into the sea about 1.5

kilometers (1 mile) south of Kursi, providing a convenient location for the miracle. Jesus instructed the man whom he healed to spread the good news of God's mercy to his gentile countrymen (Mk 5: 18–10), and the next time that Jesus returned to the Decapolis he was met by an eager crowd (Mk 7:31–37).

Tradition places the Feeding of the Five Thousand, the only Galilee miracle recorded in all four Gospels, at Tabgha (Heptapegon, lit. "seven springs") on the northwestern shore of the sea near the Plain of Gennesaret. Certain textual evidence (e.g., Lk 9:10), however, suggests that this miracle took place in the vicinity of Bethsaida, on the sea's northeastern shore. The location was a lonely, desolate spot, somewhat at a distance from any town or village (cf. Mk 6: 32, 6:36), yet within fairly easy walking distance from Capernaum (cf. Mk 6:3). While either of the two locations is possible on this account, the clues in the following episode (in which Jesus walked on water) suggest that the region of Bethsaida was the more likely location. It was the time of Passover (Jn 6:4), when the springtime grass was at its most luxuriant stage of growth (Jn 6:10). The five loaves that fed the multitude (Jn 6:9) were made from barley, the first harvest of spring. The yearly Passover celebration, a festival celebrating Israelite freedom from Egypt, fueled the Jews' longing to be freed from Roman oppression. Perhaps it was this hunger that prompted those whom Jesus fed to proclaim him to be "the Prophet who is to come into the world" (Jn 6:14), apparently a reference to the coming prophet foretold by Moses (Deut 18:15, 18:18). It is noteworthy that Elisha performed a similar miracle, multiplying fresh barley loaves for a small crowd (2 Kgs 4:42–44); like the miracle at Cana (cf. Jn 2:1–11), Jesus again surpassed his predecessor.

Jesus' disciples intended to return that evening to Capernaum by boat. Again a storm blew up, this one suddenly, as is typical in the unstable weather of springtime (Mt 14:22–33; Jn 6:16–21). While the disciples were straining to row westward against a strong west wind (Mt 14:24), Jesus came to them, walking on the water. Peter's attempt to mimic his Master was thwarted by the fierceness of the storm and his own lack of faith. The boat landed on the Plain of Gennesaret where again Jesus was met by the needy multitude (Mt 14:34–36; cf. Jn 6:25).

Jesus' travels took him to many towns and villages throughout Galilee (Mt 4:23; Lk 8:1), although only a very few other than those

JESUS' MINISTRY—SIDON TO JERUSALEM

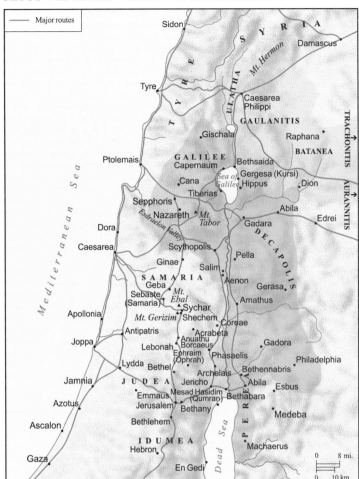

© Carta, Jerusalem

The name "Jesus," as written in Hebrew on an ossuary.

The Plain of Gennesaret with the cliffs of Arbel and the Horns of Hattin in the background.

The northern Jordan Valley, looking east toward the hills of Transjordan (the Decapolis and Perea).

hugging the northern shore of the sea are mentioned by name: Cana (Jn 2:1, 4:46), Nazareth (Lk 4:16) and Nain (Lk 7:11–17). It was at Nain that Jesus brought back to life the only son of a widow as the lad was being carried out of the city for burial. Nain was a relatively small village on the northwestern slope of the Hill of Moreh, perched at the southern border of Galilee overlooking the Esdraelon (Jezreel) Valley. Eight hundred years earlier the town of Shunem had dominated the southwestern slope of the same mountain. It was here that Elisha had raised another son, also an only child, from the dead (2 Kgs 4:8–37). By the time of the New Testament Shunem was gone, but apparently the people of Nain still remembered the prophet who had visited their mountain centuries before. Upon witnessing Jesus' miracle at the entrance to their city, the mourners exclaimed, "A great prophet has arisen among us! God has visited his people [again]!"

In addition to his visits to the Decapolis, the Gospels record only one journey of Jesus into Gentile territory: his trip with his disciples to the district of Tyre and Sidon (Mt 15:21–28; Mk 7:24–30). This journey probably took Jesus through a number of Jewish towns and villages nestled in the rugged hills of Upper Galilee, then into a very foreign land lying along the Phoenician coast. Here, as far from his "comfort zone" as Elijah was from his when he ministered to a poor widow and her son at Zarephath (1 Kgs 17:8–16), Jesus touched the lives of a poor woman and her daughter. In them, he found faith in the God of Israel among the Gentiles.

Jesus' Travels to Jerusalem. Two routes connected Galilee with Jerusalem. One passed through the Jordan Valley, crossing the Decapolis from Scythopolis to Pella, then ran along the eastern, spring-fed side of the valley through Perea, an area of Jewish settlement that, like Galilee, was governed by Herod Antipas. This route then ascended to Jerusalem via Jericho. Although the Jordan Valley was insufferably hot in the summertime, it was the preferred route for Jews who wished to avoid Samaria. The other route passed through Samaria. Jews who traveled this latter route north from Jerusalem typically spent the first night at Anuathu Borcaeus at the northern border of Judea and the second in the Esdraelon Valley, so as not to have to stay overnight in Samaria.

John records that Jesus traveled from Galilee to Jerusalem at least three times prior to his final Passover journey that led to the Cross:

- John 2:13–25 notes that Jesus overturned the money-changers' tables in the Temple precinct during the Passover festival. Many scholars suggest that John placed this event—which probably happened only once, during Jesus' last Passover journey (cf. Mt 21:12–17)—at the beginning of his Gospel in order to set the stage for an account of Jesus' life that emphasized his ministry in Jerusalem. Immediately following his narrative of the Cleansing of the Temple, John records Jesus' nighttime visit to Nicodemus, an influential Pharisee from Jerusalem who was a member of the Sanhedrin (Jn 3:1–21). Nicodemus became a follower of Jesus, advocating on his behalf during a later visit to Jerusalem (Jn 7:45–53) and helping to prepare his body for burial (Jn 19:38–42).
- Returning to Jerusalem for an unnamed festival, Jesus healed a man at the Pool of Bethesda who had been lame for thirty-eight years (Jn 5:1–17). The Pool of Bethesda was a huge public water reservoir lying just outside the city wall north of the Temple Mount. Archaeological investigation suggests that this was also a site dedicated to Aesclepius, the Greco-Roman god of healing, and no doubt served the Roman soldiers garrisoned at the nearby Antonia Fortress. Perhaps the lame man had been

hedging his bets, hoping for mercy from any deity who happened along. By healing the man, Jesus showed that he could meet the needs of not only the upper crust of Jerusalem society (e.g., Nicodemus), but also the down-and-out.

- Jesus also traveled to Jerusalem to celebrate the fall festival of Succoth (the Festival of Booths—Jn 7:1–39). It is not clear whether he made this visit after he had left Galilee for the final time before his crucifixion, or whether he returned to Galilee after the trip. In any case, his visit was made without fanfare, not wanting to take the risk of running afoul of the authorities. On the last, climactic day of the Succoth festival Jesus likened himself and his followers to fountains of living (i.e., spring) water (v. 37–38), a powerful image for the residents of Jerusalem whose own cisterns were nearly dry at the end of the summer drought. It was apparently also on this trip that Jesus healed a man who had been born blind, asking him to wash in the Pool of Siloam (Jn 9:1–12; cf. 2 Kgs 5:10).

After the trip to Jerusalem during which he was visited by Nicodemus, Jesus returned to Galilee by way of Samaria. On the second day of his journey he rested from the noontime heat at Sychar (Jacob's Well), near the ruins of the Old Testament city of Shechem, in the heart of Samaria (Jn 4:1–6; cf. Gen 33:18–19). Sychar lay beneath Mount Gerizim, the site of a Samaritan temple that had been destroyed by the Hasmonean king John Hyrcanus in 108 B.C. (Jn 4:19–20). Hyrcanus's destruction was one of many factors that had bred antagonism between the Jews and the Samaritans over the centuries (cf. 2 Kgs 17:24–41; Neh 4:1–9). Like the Jews, the Samaritans considered themselves to be the true guardians of the pure Mosaic faith, basing this belief on the ties that Abraham (Gen 12:6–7), Jacob (Gen 33:18–19; Josh 24:32) and Moses (Deut 11:26–32; Josh 8:30-35) had to the region. Jesus remained in Samaria for two days—much to the consternation of his disciples—and many believed in him (Jn 4:39–42).

Jesus' Last Year: The Way of the Cross. During the early part of his ministry, Jesus preferred to avoid the limelight that would invariably accompany messianic claims and instead simply went about towns and villages, preaching the good news of the Kingdom of God and healing people who were sick or demon-possessed. He spoke in parables to prevent anyone from jumping to conclusions about his objectives and goals (Mt 13:10–17; Mk 4:33–34), and often told his followers not to spread the word about his miracles (Mt 8:4, 9:30; Mk 3:12) or mention that he was the Messiah (Mt 16:20). Slowly, methodically and with an eye to the future, the ground was prepared and the seed sown.

Then the time was ripe. Jesus took his disciples into the region of Caesarea Philippi, in the northern reaches of Gaulanitis. This was an area where Hellenism had taken deep root among a scattering of Jewish villages, a region that represented in microcosm the Jewish Diaspora in the Roman world. The city of Caesarea Philippi (modern Banias), lying at the foot of Mount Hermon awash in the headwaters of the Jordan River, was a pagan cult site devoted to the worship of the god Pan and the Nymphs. Here Herod the Great had built a temple to the divine Caesar, Augustus, out of which a powerful spring of living water flowed. Jesus chose this context to question his disciples, "Who do you say that I am?" (Mt 16:13–16). Peter affirmed that Jesus was the Messiah, the Christ, and Jesus replied by giving him the keys to the kingdom of heaven (Mt 16:17–19). Here Jesus also mentioned the church, the first of only two times that this concept, so integral to the spread of the Gospel in the Roman world, appears in the Gospels (cf. Mt 18:17). With Peter's confession, Jesus made the first of three Passion predictions: that

"HE RESOLUTELY SET HIS FACE TOWARD JERUSALEM" (LK 9:51)

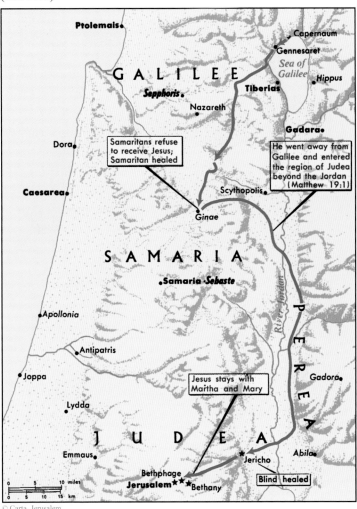

© Carta, Jerusalem

he had to go to Jerusalem, that he had to suffer and be killed, and that he had to be raised on the third day (Mt 16:21–23, 17:22–23, 20:17–19). The die was cast; the disciples, for the most part, were unwilling and afraid (cf. Mt 16:24–28).

Six days later, to confirm his role as the divine God-man, Jesus took Peter, James and John, the "inner three" of his disciples, to a high mountain where he was transfigured before them. There, in the presence of Moses and Elijah, a voice from heaven pronounced Jesus to be "My beloved Son with whom I am well pleased; listen to him!" (Mt 17:1–8). One early Church tradition places the Transfiguration on Mount Tabor, a dramatic mountain near Nazareth looming over the northeastern corner of the Jezreel Valley. Another, attested by Eusebius in the early fourth century A.D., prefers to locate this event somewhere on Mount Hermon, since Jesus and his disciples were already in the vicinity of Caesarea Philippi. If the location of Mount Hermon is correct, then Jesus' last, triumphal journey to Jerusalem can be seen as beginning here, at the farthest extent of the Holy Land. From Mount Hermon Jesus embarked on a final long, circuitous journey that took him one last time to each of the regions in which he had focused his ministry (Mt 17:24, 19:1–2, 21:1; Lk 9:52, 17:11) before cresting the Mount of Olives on the Sunday before Passover.

So Jesus "resolutely set his face toward Jerusalem" (Lk 9:51). He spent most of the winter prior to his final Passover in Perea, the "Judea beyond the Jordan" governed by "that fox," Herod Antipas (Mt 19:1–2; Lk 13:32). Here he had greater contact with the religious authorities from Jerusalem than he had had in Galilee, and it is likely that many of their confrontations recorded in the middle

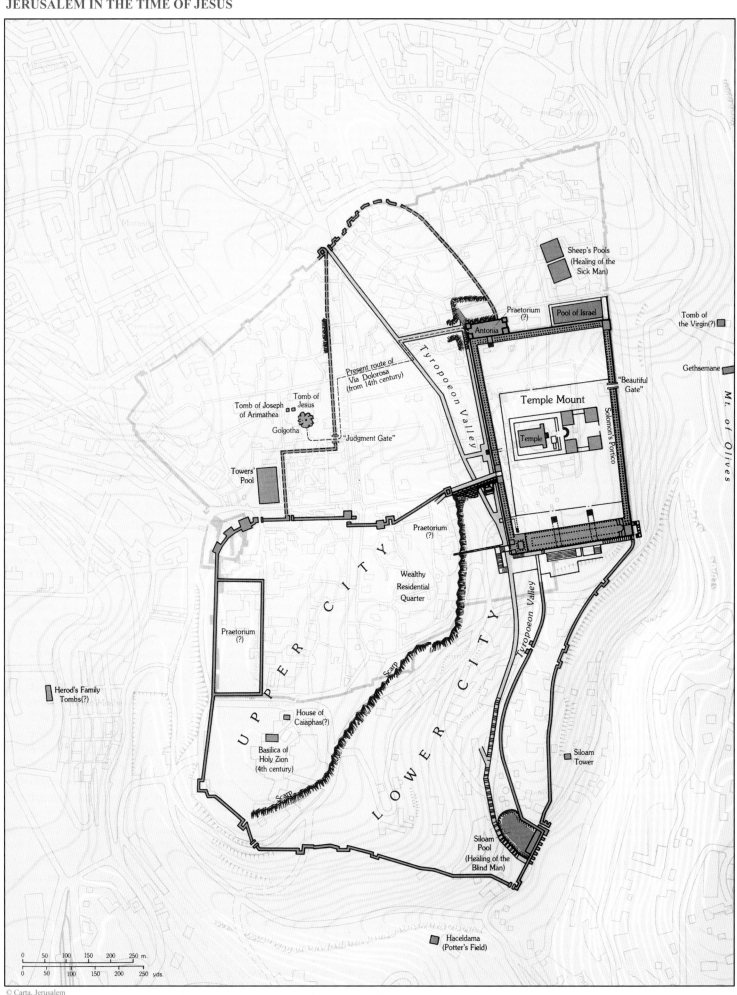

Sheep's Pools
(Healing of the
Sick Man)

Praetorium
(?)

Pool of Israel

Tomb of
the Virgin(?)

Antonia

Gethsemane

Present route of
Via Dolorosa
(from 14th century)

Mt. of Olives

"Beautiful
Gate"

Tomb of Joseph
of Arimathea

Tomb of
Jesus

Temple Mount

Golgotha

Solomon's Portico

"Judgment Gate"

Temple

Tyropoeon Valley

Towers'
Pool

Praetorium
(?)

U P P E R   C I T Y

Wealthy
Residential
Quarter

Tyropoeon Valley

Praetorium
(?)

Scarp

L O W E R   C I T Y

Herod's Family
Tombs(?)

House of
Caiaphas(?)

Siloam
Tower

Basilica of
Holy Zion
(4th century)

Scarp

Siloam
Pool
(Healing of the
Blind Man)

Haceldama
(Potter's Field)

0   50   100   150   200   250 m.

0   50   100   150   200   250 yds.

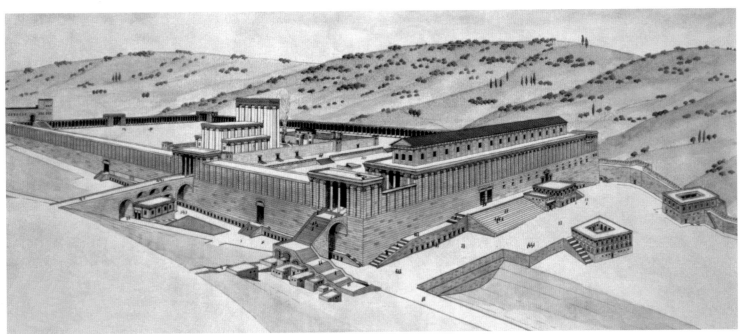

Reconstruction of the Temple Mount in the time of Herod the Great.

chapters of the Gospel of Luke would have taken place at this time, as Jesus' ministry was approaching its climax (Lk 10:25–29, 11: 14–26, 11:37–54, 13:31–35, 14:1–6, 15:1–2, 16:14, 18:18–30). Perea also provided a fitting setting for Jesus' parables of the Good Samaritan (Lk 10:30–37) and the Prodigal Son (Lk 15:11–32), since the region lay adjacent to Samaria and the Decapolis (where a man might eat with the pigs), and his audience would have often traveled the Jerusalem-Jericho road.

Jesus himself traveled up to Jerusalem from Perea at least twice before completing his final journey to the Cross. The first was to attend the Feast of Dedication (Hanukkah), which celebrates the cleansing of the Temple by Judas Maccabeus in 164 B.C. (Jn 10: 22–42). When pressed by the people to declare himself the Messiah, Jesus answered, "I and the Father are one" (Jn 10:30). Jesus' second trip was to Bethany, a small village on the eastern slope of the Mount of Olives where, in a touching scene revealing the depths of his humanity and divinity, Jesus raised Lazarus, brother of Mary and Martha, from the dead (Lk 11:1–53).

Jesus' final journey to Jerusalem, like his previous ones, took him through the oasis city of Jericho where he passed under the shadow of Herod's elegant winter palace. As a border town, a hub of routes and a market for balsam trade, Jericho was a tax-collection center where agents like Zacchaeus, under the patronage of Rome, made a fine living cheating the residents of the area (Lk 19:1–10). Jericho's wealth attracted the desperately poor as well, persons such as Bartimaeus, a blind roadside beggar (Lk 18:35–43). True to form, Jesus encountered both men and by the time he left town to climb to Jerusalem both had become his followers.

As was his custom, Jesus made the village of Bethany his home while he was in Jerusalem (cf. Mt 26:6). He spent the upcoming Sabbath there, then on Sunday morning sent his disciples to the nearby village of Bethphage to secure a colt for his triumphal ride into Jerusalem (Mt 21:1–11; Lk 19:28–36). Cresting the Mount of Olives, Jesus wept over the city, mixing tears of sorrow over its coming destruction with the crowd's cheers of victory: "Hosanna!" ("Save now!"—Lk 19:37–44; cf. 2 Sam 15:23, 15:30). Jesus entered the city from the east and then, in his strongest messianic statement yet, overturned the money-changers' tables in the Temple precinct, cleansing its courts for proper worship and prayer (Mt 21:12–17; Lk 19:45–46). Jesus spent the next day or two boldly teaching in and around the Temple courtyard, a popular place for rabbis to gain and hold a hearing—or, to lose one (Mt 21:23–23:39).

Messianic expectations ran high in Jerusalem on the eve of the Passover and the city was crowded with pilgrims from across the Roman world. Jesus' presence in the city at this time was a threat to the Temple authorities and they planned to seize him quietly, fearing civil unrest (Mt 26:1–4). Longing to celebrate the Passover with his disciples (Lk 22:15), Jesus instructed Peter and John to prepare a room for the meal (Lk 22:7–13). Tradition, as well as archaeological and literary evidence, points to a large, well-to-do home or institution on the highest point of the Upper City of Jerusalem—today's Mount Zion—as the location for the Last Supper. The setting was formal, proper and solemn (Mt 26:20–29; Lk 22: 14–23). Judas, having arranged beforehand to turn Jesus over to the Temple authorities (Lk 22:3–6), left the meal early (Jn 13:21–30).

Late in the evening, after the meal, Jesus and the rest of his disciples walked to Gethsemane ("olive press") in the Kidron Valley, at the foot of the Mount of Olives. There they sought solitude and divine strength for the events to come (Mt 26:30, 26:36–46). Jesus was arrested, abandoned by his disciples and taken back to the Upper City of Jerusalem to the home of Caiaphas, the high priest, for interrogation (Mt 26:47–57; Jn 18:1–11). Jesus was questioned first by Annas, the former high priest, and then by Caiaphas himself, who presided over a tribunal composed of members of the Sanhedrin, Jerusalem's supreme religious governing body (Lk 22:66–71; Jn 18:12–24). As members of the Sadducean aristocracy, Annas and his son-in-law Caiaphas looked unfavorably upon popular messianic unrest against Rome. Meanwhile Peter, secretly listening to the proceedings from an outer courtyard, denied three times that he knew Jesus when pressed by onlookers to identify himself (Lk 22:54–62; Jn 18:15–18, 18:25–27).

Jesus' statements before Caiaphas were seen as blasphemous (Mt 26:57–68; Jn 18:19–24), but the tribunal was not able to inflict the death penalty. For this, Jesus was taken to Pontius Pilate, the Roman governor of Judea. Pilate's official residence was in Caesarea on the Mediterranean coast, but his responsibility to suppress any hint of insurrection in Judea had brought him to Jerusalem during the Passover. Jesus faced Pilate in the Praetorium, where his accusers presented him as the "King of the Jews," an upstart bent on fostering a rebellion against the emperor (Mt 27:11–26;

Panoramic view of Jerusalem, looking southwest. In foreground, the Temple Mount with the Golden Dome of the Rock and el-Aqsa Mosque.

Lk 23:1–3; Jn 18:28–19:15). Luke's Gospel includes an additional hearing before Herod Antipas, who was also in Jerusalem for the Passover (Lk 23:6–12).

After being scourged and mocked by the Roman garrison in the Praetorium, Jesus was led through the streets of Jerusalem to Golgotha ("the Place of the Skull") where he was crucified (Mt 27: 27–56; Lk 23:26–49; Jn 19:16–30). The route of the Via Dolorosa ("Way of the Cross") can be determined only in relation to the location of the Praetorium and Golgotha. Tradition places the site of the crucifixion at the Church of the Holy Sepulchre, which at the time of Jesus' crucifixion lay outside a northwestern bend in the city wall, near a road leading into the city and in an area used as both a garden and a cemetery (cf. Jn 19:41–42). The Praetorium—Pilate's residence while in Jerusalem—may have either been within the Antonia Fortress adjacent to the northwestern corner of the Temple Mount, or in Herod's Palace in the northwestern corner of the Upper City. Because the Sabbath was approaching, Jesus was buried in a newly hewn tomb nearby (Lk 23:50–56; Jn 19:38–42).

The Resurrection took place early the next Sunday morning (Mt 28:1–10; Lk 24:1–12; Jn 20:1–10). Jesus appeared first to Mary Magdalene as she stood weeping at the tomb (Jn 20:11–18; cf. Lk 8:2; Mk 15:40, 15:47), then late that afternoon to two men on the road to Emmaus (Lk 24:13–35). Four sites have been proposed for Emmaus; the one that makes most sense geographically is in the vicinity of modern Mozah, a village in the Judean hills less than two hours' walk west of Jerusalem. Later that evening Jesus appeared to his disciples in Jerusalem, perhaps back in the Upper City (Lk 24:36–49; Jn 20:19–25), and then to them again, eight days later (Jn 20:26–29; cf. 1 Cor 15:3–8). Jesus also appeared to seven of his disciples on the northern shore of the Sea of Galilee, where he found that they had returned to fishing (Jn 21:1–3). In an act that echoed their initial call, Jesus foretold Peter's miraculous catch of fish, then commissioned him to "feed my sheep" (Jn 1:4–17; cf. Lk 5:1–11).

Forty days after his resurrection, Jesus led his disciples to the top of the Mount of Olives where, after declaring them to be his witnesses "in Jerusalem, and in all Judea and Samaria, and even to the uttermost part of the earth," he ascended into heaven (Acts 1:1–11). Jesus' earthly ministry was over; that of his disciples was just beginning.

The Garden of Gethsemane, at the foot of the Mount of Olives.

The Growth of the Early Church in the First Century A.D.

The spread of the Gospel from Jerusalem and subsequent growth of the early church must be seen in the larger context of the Diaspora, the "dispersion" of Jewish communities across the known world. While small Jewish communities existed as far west as central Italy in the first century A.D. and a strong Jewish presence still remained in Babylon, now under Parthian control, the largest concentration of Jews lived in lands in the eastern half of the Roman Empire: Greece, Asia Minor, Egypt, and Syro-Palestine. Each of these Jewish communities was centered around a synagogue and enjoyed certain privileges granted by the Romans that allowed them to maintain their Jewish identity and govern their own internal affairs. On the whole these communities were prosperous and peaceful, and desired to maintain good relations with their Gentile neighbors. The missionary journeys of the Apostle Paul and other early evangelists focused on this region, where many of these Jewish communities provided pockets of receptivity for the Gospel message. As a Jew, Paul had ready access to synagogues wherever he went and his teachings, often controversial, were met with mixed reactions. When he left one town for another, the small group of believers left behind formed the core of a new local church.

The outworking of Jesus' commission to his disciples to "be My witnesses in Jerusalem, and in all Judea and Samaria, and even to the uttermost part of the earth" (Acts 1:8) can be traced in the book of Acts and provides a convenient geographical outline of the spread of the Gospel message: first in Jerusalem (Acts 2–7), then to Samaria and the coastal plain (Acts 8–10) and finally across the Mediterranean world to Rome (Acts 11–28). Surprisingly, almost nothing is mentioned in Acts about the growth of the church in Galilee, the focal area of Jesus' ministry (cf. Acts 9:31). Moreover, Luke, the author of Acts, included only a small selection of events in his work that took place in the decade between Jesus' crucifixion and the death of Herod Agrippa I, grandson of Herod the Great, in A.D. 44 (cf. Acts 12:20–23). What is mentioned, however, is adequate to help readers determine the general nature of the challenges and opportunities that faced those who believed in Jesus as Messiah during these crucial early years, and to set the stage for the missionary journeys of the Apostle Paul into the Roman world.

"You shall be My witnesses in Jerusalem...." Most Jews living in the Diaspora maintained close contacts with Jerusalem, their spiritual home. While the journey was often difficult and expensive, many tried to make a trip to Jerusalem at least once in their lifetime for one of the three *hagim*, or pilgrimage festivals, mandated by Mosaic law: Pesach ("Passover"), Shavuot ("Weeks" or "Pentecost") and Succoth ("Tabernacles" or "Booths") (cf. Ex 23:14–17; Deut 16:1–17). During these festivals Jerusalem took on a lively, cosmopolitan air as pilgrims from across the known world crowded into the city. So it was at the first Shavuot after Jesus' resurrection, when the Holy Spirit descended "as tongues of fire" upon the disciples gathered together in Jerusalem's Upper City. The disciples began speaking in the native languages of the Diaspora Jews who were in Jerusalem for the festival, persons who hailed from lands from Mesopotamia to Rome (Acts 2:1–13). Many scholars see this New Testament "Table of Nations" as a kind of reversal of the Tower of Babel incident recorded in Genesis 11. Seizing the opportunity, Peter preached a sermon declaring Jesus the Nazarene to be "both Lord and Christ," and about three thousand hearers believed (Acts 2:14–42).

Word about Jesus continued to spread when Peter and John healed a lame man at the Beautiful Gate, probably the same gate through which Jesus had passed into the Temple precinct on his Triumphal Entry (Acts 3:1–10; cf. Mt 21:12). More miraculous healings in Jerusalem followed, to the extent that persons living in towns and villages of Judea near Jerusalem brought many who were sick and demon possessed to the disciples for healing (Acts 5:12–16; cf. Mt 4:23–24).

The early success of Peter and John in gaining converts among both native and hellenized Jews aroused the same kind of controversy that had dogged Jesus' ministry (Acts 4:1–22, 5:17–42). It culminated in Jerusalem with the stoning of Stephen—a deacon in the Christian community and its first martyr—for blasphemy (Acts 6:8–7:60). Stephen's execution unleashed a strong reaction against the church, driving many converts out of the city and into the countryside of Judea and Samaria (Acts 8:1), and others as far as Phoenicia, Cyprus and Antioch (Acts 11:19). As the church dispersed, it continued to grow (Acts 8:4).

"...and in all Judea and Samaria...." Another deacon, Philip, fled Jerusalem north through Samaria to "the city of Samaria" (Acts 8:5), perhaps Sebaste, site of the Old Testament capital city of Samaria. The city was now largely gentile, having been settled by mercenaries in the days of Herod the Great. Philip's miracles there attracted the attention of one Simon Magus, a magician who also came to believe in Jesus, although apparently through impure motives. Simon was reprimanded by Peter and John in Sebaste (Acts 8:6–24). By the second century A.D. a spurious tradition had arisen claiming that Simon Magus was the father of Gnosticism, an early heresy that claimed the superiority of a spiritual form of higher knowledge not readily available to the common man.

Peter and John traveled back to Jerusalem through the towns and villages of Samaria, preaching the Gospel to the Samaritans on the way (Acts 8:25). Philip, on the other hand, was prompted by the Spirit to travel south to a "desert" (or, "pastureland"; cf. Heb. *midbar*) road connecting Jerusalem to Gaza, Palestine's gateway to Africa (Acts 8:26). In Late Roman times this route would become an important artery in the network of paved Roman roads in the region. Somewhere along its length Philip met a eunuch, a high-ranking official in the court of Candice, queen of Ethiopia (modern northern Sudan). The eunuch, who was a Jewish proselyte, believed in Jesus and was baptized, then carried his newly found faith back to his homeland (Acts 8:26–39). For his part Philip turned north, preaching the Gospel along the coastal plain from Azotus to Caesarea (Acts 8:40). The cities of the coast, though only one or two days' walk from Jerusalem, were largely incorporated into the Hellenistic world and as such lay light-years away from the conservative hills of Judea culturally. For this reason, Philip's journey up the length of the coast was the boldest statement yet by a follower of Jesus.

One of the most vehement opponents of the church in Jerusalem was Saul, a native of Tarsus in Cilicia. Saul had been trained as a Pharisee in Jerusalem by Gamaliel (Acts 22:3, 23:6, 26:5; cf. Gal 1:11–14; Phil 3:5–6), a highly respected teacher of the Law who earlier had advocated a reasoned approach toward the growing church (cf. Acts 5:33–34).

Saul traveled to Damascus, which at the time was controlled by the Nabatean governor Areatas (cf. 2 Cor 11:32–33), to search out members of the synagogues who believed in Jesus and bring them back to Jerusalem. As he neared Damascus, Saul was blinded by a great light and heard a divine voice—the voice of Jesus himself,

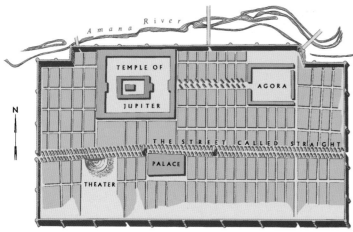

DAMASCUS IN THE TIME OF SAUL

© Carta, Jerusalem

Location of the ancient port of Caesarea.

Saul would later say (Acts 22:8, 26:15; cf. 1 Cor 15:8). Saul was led into Damascus to the home of a believer named Judas, who lived on a street called Straight, the main thoroughfare in the city. Three days later Saul was met by Ananias, a leading disciple in Damascus, who welcomed him into the growing church (Acts 9: 1–22). After spending three years in Arabia (Nabatean-controlled Transjordan—Gal 1:17), probably to sort out the ramifications of his new faith in Jesus, Saul returned to Damascus where his boldness aroused much opposition among the hellenized Jews. Returning to Jerusalem, he was welcomed into the church by Barnabas—no easy task, given Saul's previous reputation. Vehemently opposed by the hellenized Jews in Jerusalem, Saul fled for his life to Caesarea, then sailed to Tarsus, his hometown (Acts 9:23–30).

In the meantime, Peter's preaching and healing ministry had taken him to Lydda (Lod) and Joppa, two cities on the coastal plain that had historical connections to Jerusalem (Acts 9:32–43; cf. 2 Chron 2:16; Ezra 2:33, 3:7; Neh 7:37, 11:35). For Peter, a conservative man, a trip to this part of the coastal plain was relatively risk-free, since he was able to move about primarily in Jewish circles. It was quite another thing for him to go to Caesarea, to the household of Cornelius, a Roman centurion who, although a God-fearer (a Gentile who kept certain Jewish laws but was not circumcised), represented both the imperial might of Rome and the Hellenistic world generally. Yet Peter did so, after his nighttime vision of unclean animals, with the result that the household of Cornelius believed and received the Holy Spirit (Acts 10:1–48). It was thus at the Mediterranean port of Caesarea, where Herod the Great had placed Rome's most dramatic footprint in the land, that the Gospel first reached the Gentiles (Acts 11:1–18). The city would become the launching point of the Gospel to the world.

"...and even to the uttermost part of the earth." The first city to see large numbers of Gentiles come to faith in Jesus as the Messiah was Antioch in Syria, the third largest city in the Roman Empire. The church in Jerusalem sent Barnabas, an emerging leader in the church, to Antioch to assess the situation (Acts 11: 19–25; cf. Acts 4:36–37). As a Levite of Cypriot birth, Barnabas would have the proper sensitivities to understand the challenges that a large influx of Gentiles would bring to a phenomenon that so far had been primarily Jewish (cf. Acts 11:19). Barnabas in turn brought Saul from Tarsus, who readily spent a full year in Antioch bearing fruitful ministry (Acts 11:26). It was here that the believers were first called "Christians," followers of "Christos," the Messiah (the "anointed one").

The church in Antioch provided economic relief to the church in Jerusalem during a famine early in the reign of the Emperor Clau-

dius (Acts 27:30). Classical writers mention that Claudius's entire reign (A.D. 41–54) was plagued by widespread food shortages and general distress. Such offerings were gladly received in Jerusalem, where a marginal resource base ensured that the church would never become economically self-sufficient even though its members gave generously to each other (cf. Acts 2:44–45, 4:36–37, 5:1–2, 6:1, 24:17; 1 Cor 16:1–4).

The book of Acts notes the dramatic death of "Herod the king" (Herod Agrippa I) in Caesarea (Acts 12:20–23). It is known from classical sources that Agrippa I died in A.D. 44. Acts 12 then provides a firm chronological peg around which to hang other events described in the first half of the book of Acts. Agrippa's extravagant and reckless lifestyle earned him the reputation as the black sheep of the Herodian family, although once he became king he was largely faithful in observing Jewish law. Agrippa severely persecuted the church in Jerusalem, killing James the brother of John and imprisoning Peter (Acts 12:1–19).

Throughout their time of rule over Syro-Palestine, the Romans found the Jewish population of the land to be particularly difficult to control and tried various methods to enforce subservience to the emperor:

- Initially (63–40 B.C.), Rome allowed the Hasmonean family and its supporters (Hyrcanus II and Antipater, an Idumean) to remain in power in a vassal status, hoping that this buffer would win the allegiance of the people to Rome.
- Antipater's son, Herod the Great, reigned as "king of the Jews" (in reality, "king of Judea") from 40–4 B.C. He divided the land among his sons at his death: Archelaus, Antipas and Philip, although none were given the title "king."
- Rome removed Archelaus from control over Judea, Idumea and Samaria in A.D. 6 for incompetence, preferring instead to govern the province directly through a series of procurators (governors). These men were a mixed lot, though generally self-serving, cruel and corrupt, and typically ruled for three to four years before being promoted (or removed) to a position elsewhere in the Roman Empire. Of the procurators, Pontius Pilate governed the longest (A.D. 26–36), choosing in the end to commit suicide rather than face a Roman inquisition about his excesses of power. Other procurators mentioned in the New Testament are Antonius Felix, who was a freed slave (A.D. 52–60; Acts 23:24–24:27) and Porcius Festus (A.D. 60–62; Acts 24: 27–26:32).
- Agrippa I, grandson of Herod the Great, inherited the lands that had been under the control of his half-uncles Philip (who had died in A.D. 34) and Antipas (who was banished to Gaul in A.D. 39 for self-indulgence). The Emperor Claudius gave Judea,

EXPANSION OF THE EARLY CHURCH IN PALESTINE AND SYRIA

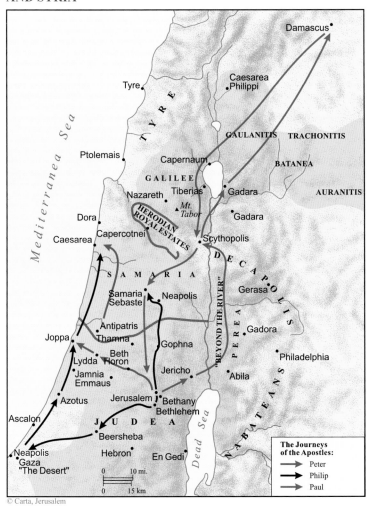

Damascus

Tyre
Caesarea
Philippi

Ptolemais
GAULANITIS   TRACHONITIS
Capernaum
BATANEA
GALILEE
Nazareth   Tiberias   Gadara
Mt. Tabor   Gadara   AURANITIS
Dora
HERODIAN ROYAL ESTATES
Caesarea   Capercotnei   Scythopolis

Mediterranean Sea

S A M A R I A
Samaria
Sebaste   Neapolis   Gerasa
Antipatris
Joppa   Thamna   Gadora
Gophna
Beth   Philadelphia
Lydda   Horon
Jamnia   Jericho   Abila
Emmaus
Azotus   Jerusalem   Bethany
Ascalon   Bethlehem
J U D E A
Beersheba
Neapolis   Hebron   En Gedi
Gaza
"The Desert"

Dead Sea

"BEYOND THE RIVER"   *P E R E A*   *D E C A P O L I S*   *N A B A T E A N S*

0   10 mi.
0   15 km

The Journeys of the Apostles:
→ Peter
→ Philip
→ Paul

© Carta, Jerusalem

Samaria and Idumea to Agrippa in A.D. 41 as well, effectively returning the Herodian royal family to full power in the land. Agrippa I extended the city wall of Jerusalem northward, enclosing a large area of suburban estates—and the site of Jesus' crucifixion—in its arc. Agrippa's brief reign (he died suddenly in A.D. 44) was the last hurrah of the Second Temple period before the nation fell to destruction.

- At the death of Agrippa I, Rome reinstated procurator rule in Judea, Samaria, Idumea and much of Galilee. A quick run of several thoroughly corrupt procurators helped to prompt the Jewish revolt that led to the destruction of Jerusalem and the Temple in A.D. 70. It was during this time that the Apostle Paul made his three great missionary journeys, as well as his trip to Rome (Acts 13–28).

- When he came of age in A.D. 48, Agrippa's son, Agrippa II, was given territory in the north and, by A.D. 61, controlled most of Perea, the eastern half of lower Galilee, and the lands that previously had belonged to Philip. Agrippa II survived the destruction of Jerusalem and remained in power until his death sometime around the year A.D. 95.

Coin of Agrippa I.

Paul's First Missionary Journey (c. A.D. 46–48). The church in Antioch had a true international flavor and its leadership, hailing from lands across the eastern Mediterranean, chose Saul of Tarsus (now known as Paul the Apostle), Barnabas and John Mark to carry the Gospel into the Roman world (Acts 13:1–3). Paul's first missionary journey took him and his companions initially to Cyprus, the homeland of Barnabas. They traveled the length of the island from Salamis to Paphos, stopping in synagogues along the way and counting among their converts Sergius Paulus, the island's Roman proconsul, or governor (Acts 13:4–12).

From Paphos Paul sailed northwest to Perga, a large port city in Pamphylia, where John Mark decided to return to Jerusalem (Acts 13:13; cf. Acts 15:36–38). From there Paul and Barnabas crossed the rugged Taurus Mountains to Pisidian Antioch, a moderate-sized city in southern Galatia lying a hard ten-days' walk from the coast (Acts 13:13–14). It has been suggested that the "perils of rivers" and "perils of robbers" mentioned in 2 Corinthians 11:26 may refer to this part of Paul's travels—or certainly something similar. Paul preached in the synagogue in Pisidian Antioch on several occasions; his message was met with mixed feelings by the Jews, but was well received by a gentile audience (Acts 13:15–49). Facing opposition in Pisidian Antioch, Paul and Barnabas fled southeast along the main trade route that connected the province of Asia with Syria, to Iconium, where his *modus operandi*—and the results—were the same (Acts 13:50–14:5).

From Iconium Paul and Barnabas continued farther southeast to Lystra. No synagogue is mentioned in Lystra, although Paul's most-beloved disciple Timothy would come from this town (cf. Acts 16:1–2). There Paul and Barnabas healed a man who had been born lame and were promptly hailed as Greek gods (Acts 14:6–18). Paul's opponents from Antioch and Iconium followed him to Lystra, driving him farther east to Derbe and the surrounding region. After making many disciples in Derbe, Paul boldly retraced his steps through Lystra, Iconium and Pisidian Antioch, strengthening the churches that he and Barnabas had planted there (Acts 14:19–23). Tracking back through the Taurus Mountains, Paul and Barnabas sailed from Attalia (modern Antalya) to Syrian Antioch where they were well received by their sending church (Acts 14:24–28).

Paul's success among the Gentiles prompted a heated discussion within the Jerusalem church about the relationship between Gentile converts and matters of Jewish law, particularly circumcision. In response, Paul and Barnabas traveled to Jerusalem for the Jerusalem Council, where they argued for the full inclusion of Gentiles into the body of believers. After much deliberation, the Council decided to place only minimal Jewish legal demands on Gentile believers; by not including circumcision among them, the way was paved for the development of a truly universal church. Carrying the Council's written decision, Paul and Barnabas, together with Judas Barsabbas and Silas, two church leaders from Jerusalem, returned to Antioch (Acts 15:1–35).

Paul's Second Missionary Journey (c. A.D. 49–52). Desiring to strengthen the churches that he had founded on his previous journey, Paul, this time with Silas, traveled overland from Antioch to Derbe. Their route followed the international highway through Tarsus and the Cilician Gates. Barnabas and John Mark, meanwhile, revisited Cyprus (Acts 15:36–41). Timothy joined Paul and Silas in Lystra and the three continued on to Pisidian Antioch, then turned north through Phrygia. Skirting Bithynia, they headed west through Mysia, a northern district of Asia, to Troas, a Roman colony that owed its prosperity to its location as the terminus of a major eastern trade route on the Hellespont (Acts 16:1–8). There the three were joined by Luke, author of the book of Acts.

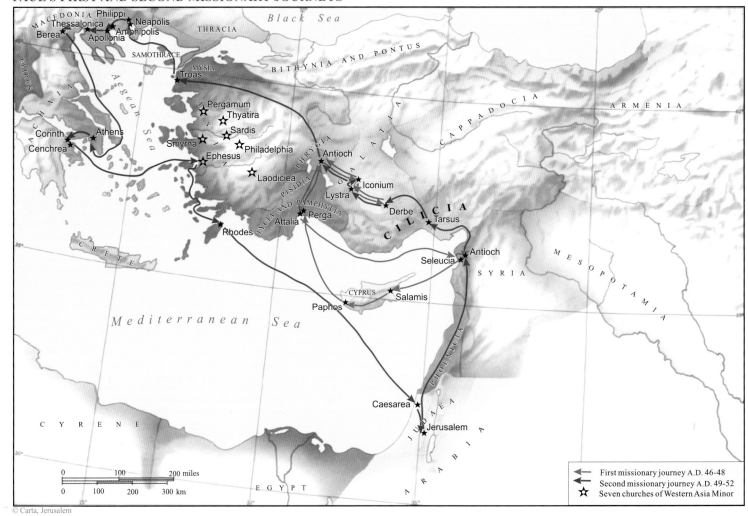

First missionary journey A.D. 46-48
Second missionary journey A.D. 49-52
☆ Seven churches of Western Asia Minor

© Carta, Jerusalem

At Troas Paul had a vision compelling him to travel to Macedonia to preach the Gospel on European soil (Acts 16:9–10), thus irrevocably altering the course of the growth of the early church. He and his companions sailed across the northern Aegean to the Macedonian port of Neapolis, then made their way inland to Philippi, a thriving city proud of its Roman heritage (cf. Acts 16:20–21). Paul's first convert in Europe was Lydia, a prosperous businesswoman and God-fearer who opened her home to Paul and his companions (Acts 16:11–15). As usual, opposition followed close at hand. As a result of a commotion that arose when Paul healed a demon-possessed slave girl, he and Silas were jailed overnight on charges that, as Jews, they were "throwing the city into confusion" (Acts 16: 16–24). That night the Philippian jailer and his family came to faith in Christ when an earthquake destroyed the cell in which Paul and Silas were being held. The following morning, upon learning that they had imprisoned Roman citizens, the Philippian magistrates urged Paul and Silas to leave the city, hoping to put the matter behind them. Paul and Silas obliged, apparently leaving Luke in Philippi to minister to its growing, much-beloved church (Acts 16: 25–40; cf. Phil 1:3–11).

Paul, Silas and Timothy traveled overland to Thessalonica where they quickly established another church, then just as quickly were run out of town by a mob who opposed their message (Acts 17: 1–9). They found greater success in nearby Berea, where a number of Jews and influential Gentiles embraced the Gospel. Leaving Silas and Timothy in Berea, Paul continued on to Athens by ship, one step ahead of the opposition that persistently dogged his path (Acts 17:10–15).

Paul's stay at Athens was relatively brief and he failed to make

The Erechtheum, on the acropolis of Athens, Greece.

significant inroads among its sophisticated population. No longer the political capital of Greece (Achaea), Athens nevertheless retained its reputation for culture and learning that it had gained in the fifth century B.C., the Golden Age of classical Greece. Paul's famous defense of the Gospel before Epicurian and Stoic philosophers of the Areopagus, in which he used the Athenian altar "to an unknown god" as a springboard to speak of the God of the Jews and the resurrected Jesus, gained a mixed reaction: some sneered while others asked for another hearing (Acts 17:16–34). It can be assumed that Paul planted a church in Athens although the New Testament fails to mention one there.

Ruins of the Temple of Apollo at Corinth, with the city's acropolis, the rocky Acrocorinth, in the background.

The climax of Paul's second missionary journey was at Corinth, the capital and main shipping center of Achaea, where he stayed for eighteen months (Acts 18:1–18). Here he was joined by Silas and Timothy. Initially Paul based his ministry out of the home of Aquila and Priscilla, Jewish believers who, like him, were tent-makers by trade (cf. Rom 16:3–4). The church grew quickly after Crispus, the leader of the synagogue, believed the Gospel message (Acts 18: 8–10; cf. 1 Cor 1:14). Many of the new Corinthian converts came from disadvantaged life circumstances while others were undisciplined extremists, and Paul remained concerned about the moral state of the Corinthian church for some time (cf. 1 Cor 1:26–29, 5: 9–13, 6:9–11; 2 Cor 7:5–16). Paul probably wrote his two letters to the Thessalonian church during his extended stay at Corinth.

Paul finally left Corinth to return home. He, along with Aquila and Priscilla, sailed from Cenchrea, Corinth's port facing the eastern Mediterranean (Acts 18:18; cf. Rom 16:1–2). After a brief stop at Ephesus where he left Aquila and Priscilla, promising to return "if God wills," Paul sailed under the prevailing Mediterranean winds across the open sea to Caesarea. Back in Palestine, he first reported to the church in Jerusalem, then returned to Antioch (Acts 18: 19–22).

Paul's Third Missionary Journey (c. A.D. 53–57). After spending some time in Antioch, Paul headed west once again to build and strengthen the churches of Asia Minor, Macedonia and Achaia. He probably began by following the same overland route into Galatia that he had taken on his previous journey, no doubt visiting for a third time the churches which he had founded in Derbe, Lystra, Iconium and Pisidian Antioch. Paul then continued west to Ephesus (Acts 18:23, 19:1). His route probably would have taken him through Colossae and Laodicea (but cf. Col 2:1); later in life, when he was in prison in Rome, Paul wrote letters to churches in these two cities (Col 1:2, 4:10, 4:15–16).

Making good on his promise to return to Ephesus, Paul remained in the city for up to three years (Acts 19:8, 19:10, 20:31; cf. Acts 18:20–21). Here he found "a wide door for effective service" (1 Cor 16:8), and used Ephesus as a base of operations to reach people from all areas of the province of Asia (Acts 19:10). The city of Ephesus was well positioned for this as it lay at the juncture of two important overland routes through Asia (one east-west, the other north-south) and was the province's main Aegean harbor. For most of his time in Ephesus Paul spoke daily in the "school of Tyrannus," perhaps renting use of the hall every midday after its normal classes had finished and after spending the mornings himself making tents (cf. Acts 18:3). Paul wrote First Corinthians (1 Cor 16:8) and probably also a prior letter to the Corinthian church (cf. 1 Cor 5:9) during this stay in Ephesus, and he may have even made a quick trip to Corinth in order to attend to some pressing matters there (cf. 2 Cor 12:14, 13:1). He also dispatched Timothy and Erastus from Ephesus to minister to the churches of Macedonia (Acts 19:22). Opposition to Paul's preaching and healing ministry in Ephesus climaxed in a riot in the city's huge theater, where the worshipers of the fertility goddess Artemis (Diana), the chief deity of the Ephesians, had gathered to exert their claim on the religious sensibilities—and economic loyalty—of the city's residents. Soon afterward Paul left for Macedonia, probably by way of Troas (Acts 19:23–20:1; cf. 2 Cor 2:12–13).

It is not possible to trace with certainty Paul's subsequent travels through Macedonia and Achaia (Acts 20:1–3). One might suppose that he visited churches that he had previously founded there. Paul stayed in Achaia—almost certainly at Corinth—for three months, and it is likely that he wrote Second Corinthians on his way there. He may also have taken a side trip sometime during this journey across Macedonia into Illyricum (Rom 15:19). It is also probable that Paul wrote his grand epistle to the Romans at this time, noting to the believers in Rome his longing to visit their city and even travel on to Spain (Rom 15:22–25; cf. Acts 19:21).

But his heart longed for Jerusalem, and so Paul retraced his steps around the Aegean to Philippi where he celebrated the Passover, then on to Troas where he again met Luke who accompanied him to Jerusalem (Acts 20:3–12). Paul and Luke threaded their way by ship through the islands off the coast of Asia to Miletus—a glorious springtime journey—where they met with the elders of the church of Ephesus for a final farewell (Acts 20:13–38). Hurrying to be in Jeru-

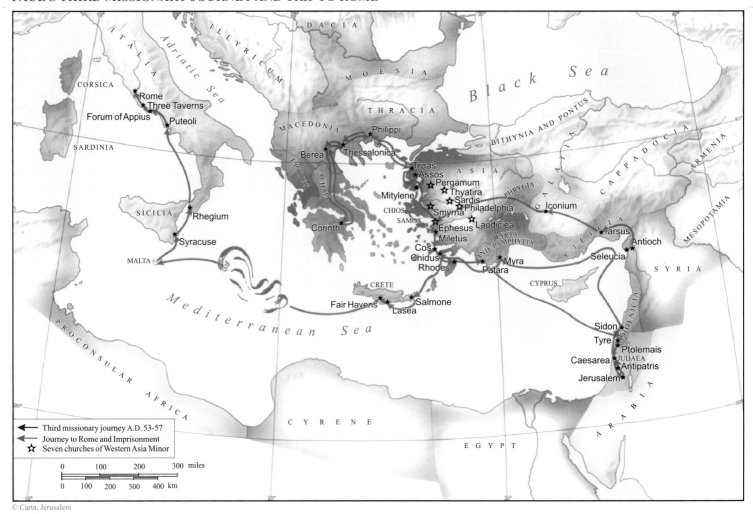

© Carta, Jerusalem

salem for the festival of Shavuot (Pentecost), Paul sailed around the southern end of the province of Asia to Patara, then straight across the Mediterranean to the ports of Tyre, Ptolemais and Caesarea. From there Paul climbed to Jerusalem, where he gave a glowing report of the spread of the Gospel among the Gentiles to James and the elders of the church (Acts 21:1–20). In the quarter century since the believers had first been empowered by the Holy Spirit at Pentecost, the church had grown with remarkable success.

Paul's Arrest and Journey to Rome (c. A.D. 59–62). On each of his journeys, Paul faced the issue of how closely Jews who were living in the Gentile world and who came to believe in Jesus should adhere to normative Jewish religious practices. Now, so as not to cause undue offense to the Temple authorities, Paul completed the proper purification rites for a vow that he had made, then entered the Temple precinct for Pentecost (Acts 21:20–26; cf. Acts 18:18). Toward the end of the festival he was falsely accused of bringing a Gentile into the Temple, thus defiling the sanctuary. Paul was arrested, gave a defense of his actions before the crowd that had gathered in the Temple courtyard, and then taken before the Sanhedrin (Acts 21:27–23:11). Hearing of an attempt on Paul's life, the Roman garrison commander in Jerusalem ordered his evacuation to Caesarea, the provincial seat of government (Acts 23:12–35). The initial leg of that journey, through the rough hills from Jerusalem to Antipatris, was made with a heavy armed guard under the cover of darkness, apparently to lessen the threat of ambush.

After a formal hearing in Caesarea, Felix, the procurator, kept Paul in open confinement for two years, in part hoping that the prisoner would bribe his way to freedom (Acts 24:1–27). When Festus,

Felix's successor, granted Paul another hearing at the beginning of his term of office, Paul exercised his right as a Roman citizen and appealed directly to Caesar (Acts 25:1–12; cf. Acts 22:25–28). King Agrippa II held a third hearing in Caesarea after which both he and Festus agreed that had Paul not appealed to Caesar, he could have been set free (Acts 25:13–26:32).

Paul, again accompanied by Luke, began his long journey to Rome under armed guard on a small trading ship heading back to its home port of Adramyttium on the west Asian coast. The boat sailed west against the prevailing winds, hugging the coast of Cilicia, Pamphylia and Lycia. At Myra, Paul was put aboard a large Alexandrian freighter loaded with over seventy tons of Egyptian wheat bound for Rome (Acts 27:1–6). It was late in the shipping season, well past "the fast" (i.e., Yom Kippur, the Day of Atonement —Acts 27:9), and the onset of sudden winter storms posed a real risk to travel on the high seas. Failing to find safe winter anchorage at Crete, the ship was caught by a violent wind and driven against the waves for two weeks until finally running aground and breaking up on the tiny island of Malta (Acts 27:7–44).

Although the ship and its cargo were lost, all of the passengers made it safely to land and spent the winter on the island. In the spring Paul continued by ship to Italy, touching briefly at Syracuse in Sicily and Rhegium on the tip of the Italian "boot" before landing at the port of Puteoli. There Paul met with believers who escorted him up the Appian Way to Rome. The book of Acts ends with Paul under house arrest in Rome, where for two years he preached the Gospel of Jesus to all who would hear (Acts 28:1–31).

Tradition, supported by some New Testament textual evidence (eg. Philem 22), holds that Paul was released from custody in Rome

THE JEWISH REVOLT AGAINST ROME, A.D. 66–70

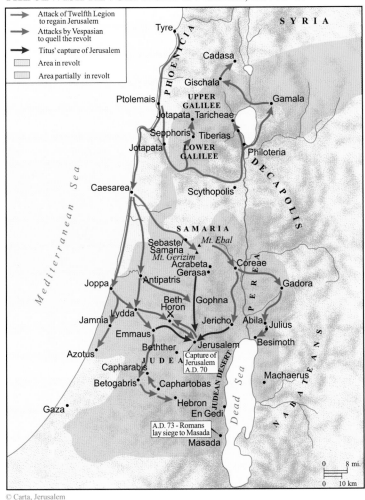

Legend:
- Attack of Twelfth Legion to regain Jerusalem
- Attacks by Vespasian to quell the revolt
- Titus' capture of Jerusalem
- Area in revolt
- Area partially in revolt

© Carta, Jerusalem

and traveled to other parts of the Mediterranean, including Crete (Titus 1:5). In his epistle to the Corinthians (c. A.D. 96), Clement of Rome noted that Paul "went to the limit of the West," which may be a reference to Spain (cf. Rom 15:23–24). A second imprisonment, probably during the reign of Nero, is implied in 2 Timothy 4:6–18. It is thought that both Paul and Peter met their deaths in Rome in A.D. 67–68 during Nero's persecution of the Christians. As a Roman citizen, Paul would have been beheaded with the sword.

The Jewish Revolt Against Rome (A.D. 66–73).

The growth of the early Church in the middle of the first century A.D. should be viewed against the backdrop of the uneasy relationship between the Jews and the cultural and military forces of the Roman Empire. Diaspora Jews lived as a minority—albeit a rather significant one—in a vast sea of Hellenistic culture and, although they were granted certain important privileges that allowed them to maintain a degree of self-autonomy, they had no desire to establish political control in the lands in which they lived. Not so for the Jews living in their historic homeland, the hills of Judea and Galilee. Here, in spite of a thin aristocratic upper crust that preferred to maintain its socio-economic position by not rocking the Roman political boat, the hope for real freedom beat strong within the heart of the vast majority of the people. The more Rome clamped down on the Jews, the stronger the desire for freedom grew, fueled by increasingly corrupt procurators who repeatedly offended Jewish religious sensitivities. The inevitable result was open revolt.

This drive for political freedom was spearheaded by the Zealots and a fanatical fringe group called the Sicarii—assassins—who resorted to kidnapping and murder to force Jewish political independence. When a majority of the Pharisees joined the Zealot cause, opposition to Roman rule gained widespread popular support. The spark that led to revolt flashed first in Caesarea with a clash between Greeks and Jews that resulted in the Jews being expelled from the city (A.D. 66). When news of this reached Jerusalem, riots there only fanned the flames. Neither the procurator Gessius Florus—who earlier had robbed the Temple treasury and now fled for his life back to Caesarea—or Agrippa II could calm the situation. When Eleazar, a leading Temple official in Jerusalem, ordered that the hated sacrifice for the emperor cease, it signaled open revolt against Rome. Seizing the opportunity, Zealot groups captured the city's strongholds and by the end of the summer all of Jerusalem was under Jewish political control. As the revolt spread, the Jews captured the outlying Herodian fortresses of Masada, Cypros and Machaerus and seized the approaches to Judea. In Galilee and on the coast the Greek and Jewish populations fell on each other savagely.

Rome's response was swift and sure. Because the procurator had no legionary troops at his disposal, the governor of Syria, Cestius Gallus, intervened. Driving the Twelfth Legion to Jerusalem, he entered the city but shortly withdrew to find reinforcements. The Jewish forces followed up by ambushing and routing Gallus's troops at the descent of Beth-horon. With the immediate threat of Roman intervention gone, the Jewish rebels established a wartime government which collected revenue, minted coins and set up military districts. Of these, Galilee, the most vulnerable, was placed under the command of Josephus Flavius, the future historian, a scholar-priest with little military experience.

Tragically, the initial rebel victories were marred by bloody political infighting among numerous Jewish splinter groups. Lacking a unified front, the Jewish forces had no real chance against the renewed Roman onslaught. Nero appointed Vespasian, his best general, to the task. Vespasian brought three full legions to Ptolemais from which he attached Galilee with a vengeance. The Roman troops easily overwhelmed Josephus's defenses in Galilee and the Jewish commander surrendered after a lengthy siege at Jotapata. By the end of A.D. 67 mopping-up operations had secured the area of the Sea of Galilee and, after a heroic Zealot stand at Gamala, Gaulanitis.

Gamala in the Golan (Gaulanitis).

Triumphal parade with Temple vessels, the Arch of Titus, Rome.

© Carta, Jerusalem

Vespasian then turned his eyes to the south, quickly overrunning Samaria and the coastal plain. To isolate Jerusalem, he marched next through Perea, capturing all but the stronghold of Machaerus. Tightening the noose, Vespasian stationed the Fifth Legion at Emmaus (modern Imwas) from which he crushed the cities of the Shephelah and Hebron. After conquering the southern Jordan Valley—including the Essene settlement at Qumran—Vespasian headquartered the Tenth Legion, together with the main body of the Roman army, at Jericho. By the spring of A.D. 69, the Jewish forces controlled only the hills surrounding Jerusalem, the Judean wilderness from Herodium to Masada, and a pocket of rocky hills around Machaerus; all access beyond lay in Roman hands.

Facing revolt in the western provinces and unrest at home, Nero committed suicide in A.D. 68. After a tumultuous "year of three emperors" (A.D. 69), the Roman army in Alexandria and Caesarea proclaimed Vespasian emperor. Vespasian's son Titus was dispatched from Alexandria to Jerusalem to finish his father's task. With a combined force of four Roman legions, Titus attacked Jerusalem from the north, the city's most vulnerable approach, in the spring of A.D. 70. The Jewish defenders, finally united in their struggle, were no match for the Roman assault. Systematically and relentlessly, the Romans breached each of the city's defenses, burning the Temple on the Ninth of Ab (28 August). The Upper City of Jerusalem held out for another month. When it finally fell, Titus ordered the entire city to be leveled with a vengeance uncharacteristically fierce even for the Romans. Only the three towers that had guarded Herod's palace remained standing; around these the Tenth Legion, assigned to guard the city, now camped. Follow-up operations took the fortresses of Herodium, Macherus and finally, in A.D. 73, Masada, after the celebrated confrontation between the Roman general Silva and the Zealot commander Eleazar.

The threefold tragedy of the destruction of the Temple, the cessation of sacrifices and the dissolution of the high priesthood shook Judaism to the core, but by focusing inwardly on the "tradition of the fathers" Jewish life found a renewed and fruitful expression through the local synagogue. The Sanhedrin reconstituted itself as the official authoritative body of Judaism, first at Jamnia (Jabneh) just before A.D. 100 and later in Galilee, and in the following centuries gave Judaism its normative, rabbinic shape through the compilation of the Mishnah. Christianity, still a fledgling movement, was affected as well. On the eve of the siege of Jerusalem the Christian community fled to Pella, in the Decapolis beyond the Jordan. With the Jerusalem

Herod's northern palace at Masada, overlooking the Dead Sea.

Remains of the Arcadian Way leading to the theater at Ephesus.

church now scattered, leadership passed to the churches in Antioch, Alexandria, Ephesus and elsewhere, a process of decentralization that eventually undercut Christianity's Jewish roots while allowing the church to adapt to local—and sometimes pagan—conditions. Partly because the Christians did not take part in the revolt against Rome, the Romans ceased viewing the movement as a Jewish sect and withdrew from it the official Diaspora privileges that it had previously enjoyed while under the umbrella of Judaism. By the mid-second century A.D., most Christians no longer hailed from a Jewish origin. For better or worse, the church was now weaned from its parent to come of age in a Gentile world.

The Seven Churches of Revelation. At the end of the first century A.D. the church faced intense persecution at the hands of Domitian, a particularly cruel emperor who insisted that all of his subjects address him as "Lord and god." The Apostle John, elderly and imprisoned on the island of Patmos during Domitian's reign, saw the ramifications of the new world that now faced the Church in a series of remarkably vivid visions which he recorded in the book of Revelation. At the beginning of his book, John addressed seven churches located in the province of Asia. He encouraged their members to be faithful in the face of persecution and warned them about dangerous heresies that threatened their existence (Rev 1:4–3:22). The problems and promises that these seven churches faced are typical of those that have confronted Christians in many parts of the world for centuries.

The letters to these seven churches are ordered in the book of Revelation in a clockwise geographical sequence starting with Ephesus.

- **Ephesus.** Strategically located on the west Asia coast, Ephesus was the political and commercial center of the region and the hub from which Christianity spread to the province of Asia and the Aegean. The island of Patmos, where John was imprisoned, lay 50 miles (80 kilometers) out to sea to the southwest. Extensive archaeological remains can be seen at the site of ancient Ephesus today, although most postdate the time of the New Testament. John commended the Ephesian church for its steadfastness, but noted that its members had lost their first love (Rev 2:1–7).

- **Smyrna.** Smyrna is modern Izmir, the third largest city in Turkey, and the ancient site is so built over today that little archaeology is possible. With a sweeping harbor and control of immensely fertile agricultural lands, first-century Smyrna felt itself to be the true center of the province and, like both Ephesus and Pergamum, claimed the title "First of Asia." The Smyrna church was commended for its perseverance in the face of persecution, and exhorted to be faithful even unto death (Rev 2:8–11).

- **Pergamum.** The ancient city of Pergamum was draped over a 305-meter (1,000-foot) high hill above a large, fertile valley and enjoyed a magnificent view of the Bay of Lesbos on the Aegean 24 kilometers (15 miles) to the west. Today the site (above the modern city of Bergama) boasts wonderful standing ruins, many of which date to the second century B.C., and is a real treat for visitors. Renowned as a center of art and literature, Pergamum was the official cult center for emperor worship in Asia. John noted the faithfulness of many in the church of Pergamum who faced unusually intense temptation—situated as they were at "Satan's throne"—but condemned those who had fallen into immorality and self-indulgence (Rev 2:12–17).

- **Thyatira**. The ancient site of Thyatira is located under the modern city of Akhisar making excavation difficult, and only meager remains have been found, none of which date to the first century A.D. Although militarily indefensible, the site was located on the imperial post road linking Mesopotamia to Syria and so developed an important role in international commerce. The residents of Thyatira were famous in antiquity for establishing highly organized trade guilds, many of which serviced workers in various types of cloth (cf. Acts 16:14). John commended the Thyatirian church for its growing faith and service, but condemned certain members who tolerated the apostate teachings of the "prophetess Jezebel" (Rev 2:18–29).

- **Sardis**. Rich in historical associations, Sardis had held strategic military and commercial value since the beginning of the thirteenth century B.C. The ancient city dominated the region of the Hermus River, the broadest and most fertile of all the river basins in Asia Minor. The extensive ruins of Sardis, located just south of the modern village of Sart, date primarily to the second and third centuries A.D., although the remains of a fourth-century B.C. temple to Artemis imitating the Artemis temple in Ephesus (cf. Acts 19:23–28) are noteworthy. John sounded a stern "wake-up" call to the apathetic church in Sardis, noting that only a few of its members had remained faithful (Rev 3:1–6).

- **Philadelphia**. Although located in an arm of the same valley as Sardis and occupying a spot on the imperial post road, Philadelphia was a second-rate city in the first century A.D. with little to boast of other than its position as a beneficiary of the financial patronage of the emperor. Today the small town of Alasehir is located on the same site, and no excavation of the ancient city has taken place. John had nothing negative to say about the church in Philadelphia. He commended its faithfulness despite its "little strength" and noted that the church faced "an open door which no one can shut" (Rev 3:7–13).

- **Laodicea**. One hundred miles (62 kilometers) upriver from Miletus (cf. Acts 20:15–38), Laodicea and its neighbor Colossae were situated at a great hub of routes, ensuring prosperity and opportunity for their residents. Laodicea was a banking center and boasted a famous medical school. The remains of the city cover hundreds of acres, but little excavation has been done. Among the finds is a sophisticated aqueduct carrying water from springs 10 kilometers (6 miles) away; unlike the hot springs bubbling up at neighboring Hierapolis and the cool springs watering Colossae, the water of Laodicea was lukewarm by the time that it reached the city. John had nothing favorable to say to the church at Laodicea. Though its members were privileged (cf. Col 4:13–16), he compared them to lukewarm water, apathetic and stale, and urged them to renew their commitment to Christ (Rev 3:14–22).

Remains of the Temple of Artemis at Sardis.